# *Coming Down the Seine*

# Lost and Found Series

*New editions of the best in travel writing—old and modern—from around the world*

*Classic Travel Writing*

**Use the Internet for FREE at all Essex Libraries**

Essex County Council
Libraries

# Coming Down the Seine

## by Robert Gibbings

Signal Books
*Oxford*
2003

This edition published in 2003 by
**SIGNAL BOOKS LIMITED**
36 Minster Road
Oxford
OX4 1LY
**www.signalbooks.co.uk**

First published in 1953
© Robert Gibbings, 1953
Foreword © Martin Andrews 2003

A catalogue record for this book is available from the British Library
ISBN 1-902669-56-8 Cloth
ISBN 1-902669-57-6 Paper

All illustrations by Robert Gibbings

Cover Design: Baseline Arts
Typesetting: Devdan Sen
Cover Image: Robert Gibbings

Printed and bound in Canada

# COMING
# DOWN
# THE
# SEINE

BY

## ROBERT
## GIBBINGS

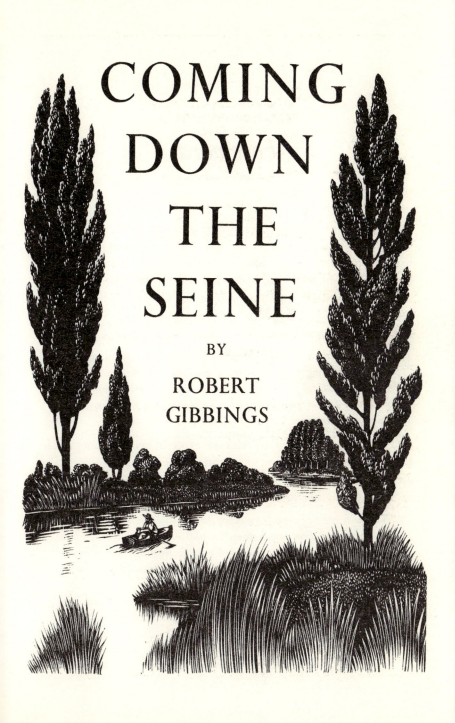

# *Foreword*

BORN IN IRELAND in 1889, Robert Gibbings spent his childhood living by the banks of the river Lee near Cork. For the rest of his life he had a love of rivers and a passion for messing about in boats. Fascinated by the wildlife he found on, under, and near the water, he also viewed rivers as endowed with a spiritual significance. In an article he published in the journal *John O'London's Weekly* in September 1953 he tried to describe his feelings:

> *I think it is the unbroken sequences of flowing water, the unchanging destinies of streams, that seem to knit a man's soul with the eternities. The rhythms of eddying pools, the rhythms of lapping wavelets, bring peace through eye and ear, emphasizing by their unceasing flow the unimportance of our passing troubles.*

His journey down the river Seine was expected to once again provide reflective tranquillity, but in this article he graphically described the dramatic reality—the timing of his adventure had coincided with a period of storms and flooding:

> *Forests were submerged to such a depth that the lower branches of the trees were torn from their parent stems. Tangled with their neighbours and carried with increasing momentum, they made their way across country until, halted by some remote obstacle, they formed a barrage that spread the cataract over a yet wider area.*
>
> *And there I was in a flat-bottomed boat the size of a hip-bath. The maelstrom rushed me here, swung me there; if I wasn't escaping the fate of Absalom under falling trees, I was having my flesh racked from me as I shot through the scarce open eyes of bridges. Again and again I had to wade waist deep through submerged thickets where brambles tore at my naked limbs.*

*Strangely enough, even in the height of the fury I couldn't but exult in the sharing of such unbridled strength and freedom.*

Despite these traumas, when *Coming Down the Seine* was published on September 10, 1953, it was an immediate success. Even earlier, Gibbings' publishers, J. M. Dent & Sons, had been delighted with a report from one of their readers who had seen a final draft of the book and described it in glowing terms:

*I thoroughly enjoyed this delightfully written book on Mr. Gibbings's latest river journey—all four hundred miles of it! While it struck me as being rather more serious in mood at times than his last book, meditative comment or philosophical aside takes nothing from and, indeed, tends to enhance the characteristically light and facile touch. No opportunity for the humorous approach is ever missed, no opening for the apt story ever escapes, no "character" ever fails to receive deft appreciation. From the source of the river to its mouth, there can be but very few places worthy of any note about which he did not find something interesting or amusing to relate, whether because of their historical importance, their artistic associations, their scenic peculiarities or their local legends, customs or industries. The dangerous nature of his journey in a flimsy little boat on the flooded river will be missed by none of his readers, despite his light-hearted way of describing it. He has captured the "atmosphere" of Paris with effortless ease—Paris of bridges, the pavement cafes, the art schools and the ateliers—which after all is not very surprising! Recurring through the book are passages of descriptive writing of great beauty, rich in imagery—writing in fact of a high order.*

But however good his writing was, Robert Gibbings was primarily an artist and he attached equal importance to the wood-engraved illustrations in his books. He was a student at the Slade School of Art from 1911 until the outbreak of the First World War. During this time he also studied printmaking at the Central School of Arts and Crafts where he was taught wood-engraving by Noel Rooke, one of the artists leading the revival of the medium in the early twentieth century. Gibbings is often described as having been a larger than life, colourful and adventurous character but he also became responsible, perhaps more than anyone, for bringing the art of wood-engraving to the attention of the general public.

Throughout his career Gibbings pursued a passionate belief that illustration should be visually integrated and harmonious with the text and not treated as a decorative afterthought. Thus his ambition was to control all aspects of design and production as the best way to achieve his goal. In 1924 he became director of the Golden Cockerel Press at Waltham St. Lawrence in Berkshire, which placed him in an ideal position to fulfil this ambition and he produced some of the finest books of the private press movement in the last century. Gibbings selected texts, creating new editions of work from the past, or working with contemporary authors such as A.E. Coppard, H.E. Bates, and E. Powys Mathers (with whom he published some rather exotic and erotic Eastern texts). As well as illustrating many of the books himself, he commissioned wood-engravings from leading artists of the period including John and Paul Nash, David Jones, and Eric Ravilious. Produced in limited editions, the type for the books was set by hand and printed on damped hand-made paper.

Cockerel books were of high quality and appealed to collectors around the world, but particularly in America. With the Depression in the 1930s, the market for such luxury editions slumped, and Gibbings was forced to sell the press in 1933. Later, he attempted to bring these ideals to the world of the popular paperback, both as an author and illustrator, and as art editor for the Penguin Illustrated Classics in 1938. Eventually, after a short period as a teacher of wood-engraving and book production at the University of Reading, he achieved remarkable success with books that he wrote, illustrated, and designed, working in close collaboration with his publisher J. M. Dent & Sons. These books made him a best-selling author in both Britain and America and were sold all over the world.

The first was *Sweet Thames Run Softly* (1940), for which he hand-built a boat, towed it to near the source of the river and then meandered downstream, taking notes of his experiences and observations and making sketches for his wood-engravings. Although it was never intended that he should write a series of books, the formula was so successful that there was a demand for more and from then on he made his living from writing and published six more books before he died in 1958. For his last book he returned to the river Thames; the title, *Till I End my Song* (1957), appropriately completed Spenser's famous quotation.

Gibbings' gregarious nature ensured he had a wide circle of friends and associates in the art world of the time. Of greatest significance was his close personal relationship with Eric Gill, and their working collaboration culminated in the production of *The Four Gospels*, published by the Golden Cockerel Press in 1931 and considered to be a masterpiece of book design and printing. His social circle also encompassed figures from the worlds of music, literature and the theatre. But there were many other dimensions to his life. As well as being a painter and sculptor, he was recognized as a natural historian, not in an academic way, but through his life-time passion for the outdoor life, his fascination for wildlife and his remarkable powers of observation and description. Given his love of nature it is perhaps not surprising that Gibbings was a founder member of the British Naturist Movement. He was a sensualist, always eager to throw off his clothes and embrace the sun—often only retaining his favourite wide-brimmed panama hat with a band of threaded shells from the South Seas. His friend, the author Hugh Walpole, described him as "...like the reincarnation of William Morris, huge and burly with bright blue eyes and a beard. He is a great nudist, very charming, honest."

Above all, Gibbings was a great communicator—a brilliant public speaker, he also broadcast on radio and appeared on television in its pioneering days. Through his books, talks, journalism, and broadcasts he did much to popularize the subject of natural history.

Gibbings lived life to the full and was a traveller and adventurer. He journeyed around the world seeking material for his books and wood-engravings—often to exotic places. He spent two years living with the people of Polynesia and sailed between the islands on a masted schooner; he sat on the bottom of the ocean off Bermuda drawing (on a plastic material called xylonite) the fish swimming around him. This episode became the basis for his book *Blue Angels and Whales* published by Penguin Books in 1938. Closer to home, after he floated down the river Thames, he went on to explore the rivers Wye, Lee, and of course the Seine, enjoying the landscape, history, folklore, food and wine, and most of all, the people he met on the way.

Gibbings began his research for *Coming Down the Seine* early in April 1951. He established himself in a flat belonging to some friends in the

Boulevard Raspail in the Montparnasse district of Paris—an area well known to him and liked by him for its association with artists. A week or so later he was joined by his secretary and companion, Patience Empson, and they travelled together to Dijon to investigate the source of the river Seine in a valley of the Côte d'Or. No mention of Patience Empson is made in the book, but in fact she accompanied him for most of the journey. At the beginning of July they travelled to Troyes to take possession of a small rowing boat and once afloat their adventure began. Patience later described the flood waters as looking like a great sea punctuated by the odd tall tree and telegraph pole. Bridges seemed like isolated humps but offered a dry place to sleep. Patience was acutely aware that at night she was sharing a place of refuge with many small creatures—Gibbings slept on the boat!

The journey down the river provides a central thread to the book but Gibbings, as in his other books, used this as a device that allowed him to go off at tangents and discuss a whole range of diverse subjects, often taking the reader to other parts of France and including reminiscences of his life in Ireland. All the episodes mentioned in the book are based on actual events, but the order in which they happened and the exact circumstances have been manipulated and changed to suit the structure of the narrative.

The ingredients are rich: history, folk stories, anecdotes, notes on artists and painting, sensitive and often lyrical description of landscape and wildlife and also cityscapes and people—a colourful patchwork of thoughts, ideas, and observation. As always, Gibbings took research for the book very seriously. Historical notes and aspects of natural history were meticulously checked in reference books. His amazing ability to retain information and his enquiring mind meant that he absorbed facts and details from the discussions he had with people he encountered. Often he checked out the details later, entering into lengthy correspondence with experts, societies, and authorities to confirm the accuracy of his material. Much of his "research" took the form of a less academic process, engaging folk in chat in the comfort of bars, an environment in which Gibbings was in his element. A great talker and listener, he had the gift of drawing out colourful anecdotes and stories from the people he met, which he then reworked for his books; in *Coming Down the Seine* he describes his technique:

*There is for the author an urgency in "getting things down" while they are still vivid in his brain. Life passes with such kaleidoscopic changes that unless a word, a thought, a phrase, is recorded almost as it is born, it is lost. That at any rate is my experience. It is no good saying to myself, I'll write that down in the morning. By next morning it is gone forever.*

*Here I will confess to a little bit of play-acting on my part which has got me over a few such difficulties in Ireland. With stories flying fast and furious of an evening, the only thing I could do was to develop "a bit of weakness," or maybe "a chill." This would necessitate hurried exits from the scene of poetic narrative. "Sorry, boys," I'd say, with my hand to my waistline, "I'll be back in a minute. Don't tell another story till I come back," I'd say, and then I'd rush upstairs to my room and scribble like mad. And after I had come down again and there had been another good story, I'd rush off once more. "My God, isn't the poor fellow bad?" I'd hear them saying as I hurried off.*

While gathering the material together and making visual as well as written notes, Gibbings would perhaps write an occasional descriptive passage but otherwise left the formal writing until he returned to London. Despite his apparently flowing and conversational style, he really had to work hard at writing. He would produce numerous hand-written drafts, checking detail and adjusting the form and language until he felt satisfied. The hand-written script was typed out by Patience; two or three versions would be produced and corrected, Patience acting as a careful editor, offering criticism and suggestions. These typed versions would then be cut and pasted together with proofs of the engravings to form a dummy of the complete book. This was an activity that Robert and Patience particularly enjoyed. It was an extremely important part of the design process, as the dummy would become a final specification for the printer. It was also immensely satisfying; Patience recalled with pleasure spreading the material out on the floor of Gibbings' flat in London, cutting and pasting. Because the books were rarely in the form of a continuous narrative, Gibbings was able to shuffle the text around until he found the right balance of theme and ideas, often rearranging the sequence of the illustrations, pages and even chapters. He then worked at linking the sections to give the book its final, coherent form. Thus the books developed in an almost organic way.

Gibbings produced fifty-seven illustrations for this book—each one meticulously engraved by hand into a block of wood. Wood-engraving is particularly suited to book illustration, balancing and printing well alongside metal type. It is, however, a slow and painstaking process. Gibbings would take a pencil drawing and re-draw the image in ink. A photographic negative was taken of the image and exposed onto the surface of a small block that had been coated with a light-sensitive substance. Gibbings could then engrave into the surface of the block, following his drawing and cutting out and lowering parts of the block he did not want to print, leaving his image as a raised surface. Often prints are taken from the original block, but to avoid damage and wear of the unique original woodblock, perfect metal duplicate blocks (electrotypes) were made for use on the large industrial presses that were needed to print Gibbings' books.

Considering the precision and delicacy needed to produce such small and detailed images, it seems remarkable that Gibbings was such a large man—over six feet in height and for much of his life over eighteen stone in weight! Working on such a small scale and in black and white frequently frustrated Gibbings; he longed to be able to splash out in colour. In *Coming Down the Seine*, he continually returns to the theme of painting and painters, and for his next book, *Trumpets from Montparnasse* (1955), he returned to Paris to set up a studio and paint.

To celebrate the publication of this book a dinner party was held at the Hind's Head Hotel at Bray in Berkshire. A special menu was printed listing sumptuous dishes and the wines, which flowed liberally: "Bâtard Montrachet, 1950, followed by a Château Latour, 1924, and ending with a toast, 'Success to the Seine,' with Château Filhot, 1945."

Gibbings' writing style might seem somewhat old-fashioned today and his work now has the charm of a period piece, describing aspects of a world long gone. Visitors to modern-day Rouen, for instance, would be hard pressed to recognize the war-ravaged city that Gibbings described, while the advent of the motorway network has left little of the Seine's barge culture intact. But if Gibbings provides a historical picture that remains fresh, much of what his work contains is also timeless. Most of all, his love for *la France profonde*, the France of small villages, cafés, and good food will be shared by many modern-day readers, and for this reason, as well as for its delightful illustrations, this book should be essential reading for travellers in France today.

*Martin Andrews*
*Reading, 2002*

Martin Andrews is the author of *The Life and Work of Robert Gibbings* (Primrose Hill Press, 2002).

# CHAPTER ONE

SHE was pale and cold when I saw her there beside the source, with no more clothing on her than a chaplet of lily leaves about her head and a bunch of grapes in her lap. Small wonder if she was chilly, for she had been sitting there for the greater part of a century. It was in 1867, in the reign of Napoleon III, that the people of Paris decided to erect this monument to the Seine, "the river to which Paris owes its ancient prosperity."

How charming these French statues can be! Unlike the white marble beloved of sculptors and their patrons in England, and so suggestive of nakedness, the grey limestone of France soon takes on a mellowing patina, and the nymphs and satyrs blend as happily with their surroundings as if, alive and nicely bronzed, they were scampering through the brake. I am always sorry for those figures that we see on the monuments of London, figures such as decorate the Albert and the Victoria memorials: I can only think of them as men and women who for a few shillings have taken off their clothes and struck a pose symbolic of Virtue and the Empire.

The Seine rises in a valley of the Côte d'Or, some twenty miles to the north of Dijon. Sequana, goddess of the river for over two thousand years, sits there in her grotto with one of the many sources bubbling at her feet. Before her a mirror-like pool is framed with flowering cresses and rushes, forget-me-nots, buttercups and ragged robin, and from the pool there flows a tiny stream scarce wider than your boot. To the right of the goddess another rillet issues from the ruins of a Roman temple. Unlike the ancient Gauls, who took no thought to shelter their divinities, the Romans, after the conquest of France by Julius Caesar, built sanctuaries in which to house the statues of their gods.

Archaeologists tell us that here, where only a few carved stones now remain, there was once a shrine, ornate with Corinthian columns, mosaics, and frescoes, and that pilgrims came in numbers to seek healing or other benefits of the goddess Sequana. Numerous votive offerings, models in stone or bronze of the afflicted part of the body, or small carvings of fruit or animals as gifts to the goddess, have been found on the site and are now in the Dijon museum—legs, arms, breasts, some carefully and realistically modelled, others mere token presentations. There is an image of a man with a tumour behind an ear, there is another of a girl who is blind. Perhaps the most important of all the discoveries was a bronze figure of Sequana herself: eighteen inches in height, crowned and in Grecian dress, she stands on the deck of a galley, with hands outstretched, smiling a welcome to those who seek her blessing. As on many other votive ships found in the neighbourhood, the prow of her vessel carries the head of a water bird, an emblem akin to the goosehead or *cheniscus* once mounted on the bow or stern of a Roman vessel.

It was early summer when I visited the source; the roadside was vibrant with the colours of flowers, the air exultant with the songs of larks and the chitterings of cicadas. At every step of the mile that leads from the main road into the valley there was a new surprise. White and yellow rock roses clustered on the edge of the track, gentian-blue spikes

of viperine were thick as delphiniums in a garden, golden vetches straggled among magenta orchids, lilac scabious and deep blue columbines: the plume-hyacinth, like a purple sea anemone, appeared among the roadside grasses: cornflowers and scarlet poppies lit the apple-green of young wheat in a gently undulating field.

I made my drawing of Sequana to a mixed accompaniment of tinkling cowbells and the shouts of a raucous voice that hurled constant imprecations at some unfortunate animal. Then I sought refreshment at a nearby cottage that bore the sign "Café".

"Mais oui, monsieur, une omelette," said the enormous woman with rolled-up sleeves who came to greet me from the field below the house. There was no doubt who had been addressing the horses. Her voice was as deep as her body was broad, and the limbs on her would have suited Goliath. I gathered that her husband was in hospital. But whatever the strength in those thick arms, her touch with the frying-pan was light. She had a good hand, too, with the cheese, made from the milk of the goats that grazed beside her garden. My appreciation of her cuisine was momentarily interrupted when of a sudden she burst through the half-open door of the house and rushed on to the terrace where I sat, cracking a long savage-looking whip and shouting: "Voleur! Voleur!" Intent on my own appeasement, I hadn't noticed a cat that, with some morsel purloined from the kitchen, had crept under my chair.

Peace reigned again in the valley. Wild strawberries and cream followed the goat's-milk cheese. A thrush appeared on the close-cropped grass and picked a worm from the soil. It shook it a couple of times, pecked it and then left it writhing on the ground. A few yards away it brought another to light, and treated it in the same way. It was only at the third attempt that it found one suited to its taste and swallowed it. All epicures in France, I thought. And then, reflecting on worms, I remembered trout fishing in Ireland and the trouble we would take to find the small red-and-white ringed brandlings that inhabited manure heaps, and how before putting them on the hook we would have to clear their complexions by keeping them for a few days in moss, for even a cold-blooded fish can tell at a glance if the flavour is likely to please.

The thought of trout recalled me to the river—a good meal often affects the memory—so I paid my bill, said goodbye and made my way along the path that follows the first adventurings of the Seine. Before I was out of sight Madame was again with her plough and horses, turning over the dark soil between the ridges of potatoes. "Allons! Allons!" she called, and the cracking of her whip seemed to split the air.

Coursing its way among thorns and thistles, through small meadows misty with harebells, tunnelling through a scrub of hazel, oak, privet and poplar, the rivulet gathers strength. Trickles on either side hurry to meet it, and soon, above the chorus of bird song and the rustling of leaves and reeds in the valley, one hears the first whisperings of a river. In the long grass beside a streamlet that crossed the path were several young frogs, two of them bright yellow in the sunlight, a third momentarily dark in colour from resting in a shadow—their power of colour change seems second only to that of fish. As I watched them leaping into deeper cover at my approach, the notion came to me that with all man's ingenuity he cannot make a frog, yet a female frog with but little outside help can make hundreds.

In the same stream I noticed what, but for the water, might have been an African kraal seen from a passing plane. On the upper surface of a broad stone was a cluster of miniature huts, each one about the shape and size of an English cowrie shell. But instead of being single shells, each dwelling was constructed of a dozen pin-head fragments of stone, arranged in three lines of four, from end to end. No units of mosaic laid by the hand of man ever fitted better. And under each curved roof was a minute slug-like creature, the pupa of a caddis-fly. One day a magic wand would change these Cinderellas of the stream into fairy princesses with gossamer wings, and they would dance in the noonday sun.

Scarce a mile from its source the river had been deflected through a large rectangular basin of cut stone, roofed with tiles, the first of innumerable *lavoirs* along its banks, where women kneel and scrub and doubtless gossip. In France they prefer to launder in running water and think the wash-tub far from sanitary. I asked my way of a handsome young woman whom I met as she was pushing a barrow of dirty clothes towards the wash-house. She put down her barrow and walked back with me a couple of hundred yards to point out a narrow track beside the river. I apologized for taking up her time. "There are many minutes in a day," she said, smiling. It was the first of a thousand kindnesses that were shown to me on my journey. From the source of the river to its mouth I might have been in Ireland the way they helped me on my travels. I might have been in Ireland, too, the way they refused any token of my gratitude.

# CHAPTER TWO

BEFORE I reached the source of the river I had spent a few days in Dijon, a town of richly coloured, steep-pitched roofs and silent, shadowed courtyards. At every turn I encountered gargoyled buildings, at every corner a turret or a tower. Little seemed to have changed since medieval times: it would have been no surprise to meet ladies in wimples on the narrow pavements, or to hear the clatter of knights in armour on the cobbled streets. Today the town claims to be the gastronomic capital of France. Its *Jambon aux champignons*, its *Coq au vin*, its various renderings of pike, are thought to be unsurpassed, while of course the *Escargots de Bourgogne* are epicurean: not that I grow ecstatic about snails myself, even when they have been fattened on flour and then starved for a week before cooking. One evening in the town the *patron* of a restaurant was helping me to choose my dinner.

"Escargots," he suggested.

"No," I said, "I don't much care for them."

"Then you have already eaten them?"

"Only once," I said. "That was enough. They were like leather."

He held up his hands in horror. "But where?" he asked. "In Paris," I said.

He seemed shocked. Something must have been wrong. Was it a good restaurant in Paris? Paris wasn't Dijon, of course. He went on to tell me that when cooked in butter, with garlic and onion and garnished with parsley, snails were "exquis, délicieux." Then he had an idea. Might he order one for me, just *one*? There would be no charge. He would like me to try one, just one?

The order was passed to the chef with the added instructions that special attention was to be paid to the cooking. The chef sent back for confirmation. One snail seemed a strange order, even from a foreigner.

In due course the creature arrived, solitary on its plate. Beside the plate were laid a pair of silver tongs and a small two-pronged fork. The *patron* returned also. Yes, that was right, he said. Take the shell in the tongs and extract the animal with the fork. Afterwards drink the butter from the shell, or if preferred pour it into a spoon. Ah! That was perfect, just like a Frenchman. What did I think of the flavour?

"To be honest, not very much," I said. "Not nearly as good as an oyster."

He bent down and whispered in my ear. "I don't like them very much myself."

It was one night during my stay in Dijon that I dreamt I was again in England and staying in the house of a friend, and it seemed that she had called to me to come downstairs to her help. I found her in the corner of a paved kitchen or scullery—I was particularly conscious of the paving because on it, running here and there in a slow bewildered sort of way, was a mouse, the cause of my friend's alarm. Normally she would have had no fear whatever of such a creature: her instinct would probably have been to catch it and set it free out of doors. But now in my dream she begged me to kill it, and it seemed that I had a long thick stick in my hand with which I made repeated efforts to hit the little animal. It wasn't as if I tried to strike it in the usual way, it was with definite downward jabs that I did my best to destroy it. And then I woke up, and an hour or so later I went into the town, and I had gone but a short distance from the hotel when I saw on the *pavement* a dead mouse, its belly squashed by what could only have been the downward jab of a heavy stick.

I make no claim to occult powers, though like a girl who once said to me: "I'm the kind of girl that things happen to"—and I wasn't surprised—I seem to be the kind of boy to whom odd incidents occur. In this same summer of which I write I visited Versailles. It is true that many years ago I had read *An Adventure*, by the Misses Moberly and Jourdain, which told how these apparently prosaic middle-aged ladies had been transported into the gardens of the Petit Trianon as they had been in the time of Marie Antoinette, seeing workmen and officers in the costume of that period, seeing doors and pathways and houses that no longer existed. I had read their book but forgotten it. That particular day in the gardens I had gone through the palace and I had walked through the park and looked at the fountains, the *Bassin* of Apollo, the *Bassin* of Flore, the *Bassin* of Ceres, the *Bassin* of Neptune, and many others. And eventually I had come to the Temple of Love. But the day was hot and my legs had grown weary, and I wasn't taking all the historical interest in the subject that I ought to have done. Love or no love, what I wanted then was some sort of vehicle that would take me to the town. And so I followed the path that, passing through the gardens of the Trianon, would lead me to the *station de voitures*. The day was

heavy and oppressive, the fourteenth of August to be exact. I met no one on the path, but as I came into the small formal garden to the east of the Trianon I noticed two girls crossing the path a little way ahead of me. I wasn't too tired to remark that the nearer of the two was wearing a blue skirt with a large white-flowered pattern on it, and that the general effect was attractive. On my left was a strip of grass with a number of trimmed shrubs growing from it, and the girls stepped on to the grass and passed between the second and third of the shrubs. I cocked my eye sideways to see them emerge on the other side. I waited a moment, several moments. Then, mystified by their non-appearance, I too stepped on to the grass and looked behind the shrubs. Not a sign of them, not a single sign, and a thick hedge bounded that garden.

I found a horse-drawn chariot and drove into the town. "Did you ever hear of people appearing and disappearing at the Château?" I asked the old lady who served me with a light repast.

She stared at me a moment. "I have never seen anything myself," she said solemnly, "but I have often heard of 'les fées du Trianon'." And she added: "There are some who cannot live in Versailles: they say the air is too heavy with the past."

I could speak of other queer incidents too, but instead I must get down to liquid facts and tell how, in answer to an invitation from Monsieur Louis Jadot, I travelled twenty-five miles south from Dijon and visited Beaune, the centre of the Burgundy wine trade.

"We will go for a little drive," said Monsieur Jadot when he came to my hotel with his car. "It is good that you should see first our precious hillsides." Precious hillsides! Slopes of the Côte d'Or: villages with names from a poet's encyclopaedia—Savigny, Volnay, Meursault, Santenay. Indeed I was glad to see them.

"Every hectare gives its special flavour," said Monsieur Jadot as we followed the contours of the hills. "The soil may be the same but some vineyards are better drained than others and some get more direct sunshine. It all affects the wine."

I should like to have told him that the same brand of Irish spuds grown in adjoining fields could vary vastly in bouquet, but not being sure of the breadth of his poetic vision I thought it better to suggest that even on a girl's head the small curls towards the back of her neck have a different quality from the long strands that grow on her scalp. He appreciated this comparison and went on to remind me that even from the same vineyard wines varied from year to year. I knew this, and in my turn reminded him that from the same parents children of different years varied, which of course he also knew. We were getting on well. He pointed to three adjoining vineyards, two of them side by side on the same hill, the third just below them on a gentler incline. "We will sample wines from those three when we get back," he said.

Leaving the lower vine-covered slopes we climbed into wild rough country, bleak terraces of limestone alternating with scrub and unkempt woodland. A buzzard hovered overhead. "It is their domain," said Monsieur Jadot. In the few villages through which we passed, stone archways, stone staircases and variegated tiles seemed in keeping with the sturdiness and gaiety of the inhabitants. "It is country that few but Burgundians know," he said. "It is country that all Burgundians love."

I remarked that the people of the neighbourhood seemed cheerful. "If trouble comes, you can't avoid it," he replied. "Smile anyway. That is their philosophy."

Now and again, emerging from the trees that curtain those uplands, we would see mile upon mile of vineyards stretching away before us to the south—vineyards of "prestigious evocation," as I learnt from an atlas of French wines, written in English. The same book informed me that the wines of Clos Vougeot are "full of spirit, ample, with superabundant vigour, of a rosy colour, supremely digestive, and tonic, presenting themselves to the palate in a manner in which the olfactory sense and the tongue, with a quiet and silent joy, analyse one after the other, the perfumes artfully mixed up, vying with one another, of liquorice and truffle, violets and wild mint."

From one point of vantage, looking south-east, we could see in the far distance a long range of hills, the Jura Mountains, and beyond them, faintly, the white summit of Mont Blanc. Then our road took us again into the valley, where the ordered ranks of vines lay about their châteaux. As we passed through Pommard on our way back to Beaune, Monsieur Jadot remarked that we should have ample time to visit the cellars before dinner.

Unaccustomed to the ways of *vignerons* it came as no small surprise to me, as I walked through the streets of Beaune with my host that evening, to see him stop, bend down and, after turning a key in a lock, open a pair of rusty hatches that lay embedded in the pavement. It was another surprise when I looked into the cavity thus exposed and saw not, as one might expect, a rickety ladder with a heap of coal or a few faggots at its foot, but a stately flight of stone steps leading to arcaded cloisters. Monsieur Jadot's invitation to descend, accompanied by a gracious bow, seemed almost superfluous—a natural inclination had come upon me. At the foot of the stairs surprise gave way to other emotions. I became aware not only of a warren of arches but of the generous bellying forms of casks, line upon line of them, tier upon tier, on either side, stretching away into the darkness. No lack of interest in *these* "long straight roads of France!"

Monsieur Jadot lit a candle that stood in a metal cage and handed it to me. He lit another for himself and then, like two penitents holding our tapers, we proceeded through the dark damp vaults—in Burgundy they like their cellars damp, in Bordeaux they prefer them dry. He carried with him a hammer to knock the bungs from the casks, and a glass tube, a pipette, to draw off samples of the wine. He had handed me also a small saucer-like vessel of silver, richly embossed and highly polished within—a *tastevin*. I soon discovered that the light reflected from its bosses and dimples, passing through the wine, enabled one to observe the colour of the liquid with far greater judgment than if a mere glass of it had been held to the light. We sampled the wine from the three adjoining vineyards which he had shown me. Although all were of the same year, one was a little more "brittle" than the others, another promised more "body" than its fellows. We sampled as well the produce of other vineyards, of varying years. Some were children that needed nursing, others were fully grown and ready to go out into the world. Monsieur Jadot, the expert, did not swallow what he tasted; instead, after a full trial by nose and palate, he spat with exquisite precision. For myself, I saw no reason for this refinement and enjoyed my tasting none the less.

I have always had a horror of the fate of Korah, Dathan, and Abiram. The idea of the earth opening and swallowing, and then slowly squashing one to death, has terrified me ever since as a child I heard some monstrous sermon on the subject. But in Beaune it seemed to me that if the earth did behave in that preposterous way one might well escape the worst, and even find some compensation for the insult, for the foundations of the town are such a maze of cellars that it would be hard luck indeed if one of them did not interrupt the descent. Walking through almost any street of the town one sees the unobtrusive metal plates let into wall and pavement; doorways that need no magic words to open into treasure caves, locks that need no oil from the Sesame plants of India. "Open Sesame!" No, only a small key is needed. They say that the red wines of Burgundy are food as well as drink. In such surroundings one could surely hold out for a few days without discomfort.

St. Vincent, of Spanish birth and after whom the south-west promontory of Portugal is named, is the patron saint of wines in France. Why he was chosen for this office no one seems to know, though it has been suggested that his name, Vin-cent, may have had a bearing on the matter. In an old coloured engraving he is shown as a young man with radiant halo, clad in vestments of wine colour and gold. In his right hand is the green palm of victory, in his left he is holding up a bunch of grapes. Behind him on one side are trellised vines; on the other side a lady quite naked is treading grapes in a vast tonneau. At first sight I wondered at the lady's immodesty in such company, but since then I have been told that at one time it was the custom for those treading the grapes to take off not only their sabots but the rest of their clothes as well, and then to plunge about, waist deep, among the grapes. Any stray

bacteria that they might carry with them into the vats would be killed by the subsequent fermentation of the juice. Nowadays, of course, such methods are forgotten. I am not old enough to say if the bouquet has suffered accordingly.

By way of contrast to this happy subject, it was another St. Vincent, this time of Beauvais, who summed up the pains of eternal damnation in these words:

*Nix, nox, vox, lacrymae, sulphur, sitis, aestus;*
*Malleus et stridor, spes perdita, vincula, vermes,*
which, being translated, means:

*Snow, night, wailing, tears, sulphur, thirst, fire;*
*Hammering and screaming, hope lost, fetters, worms.*
Enough to keep any man sober.

# *CHAPTER THREE*

ABOUT fifteen miles downstream from the source of the Seine lies the village of Aisey, and there at the miniature Hôtel Roy I had all the epicurean delights I could wish for. It was symptomatic of the hospitality of that house that the front door should open directly into the kitchen. There at all hours of the day Monsieur Chrétien, the *patron*, with rosy face and bright blue eyes, in the full regalia of a chef, seemed more than busy. But that did not mean that he hadn't moments for conversation. Even if he was spinning new potatoes in a frying-pan on the kitchen range, or composing some special sauce in a bowl, there was always time for a long-drawn "Ah!" of appreciation if I mentioned breadfruit, or an emotional "Oh!" if I spoke of avocado pears, for he also had spent some time in the tropics. There were intervals when at greater length he would lament the good old days when he could give his clients *Coq au Chambertin* and not just *Coq au Bourgogne* as the prices forced him to do today. Of course, it was a good Bourgogne, but even so—and then he would hold up his hands and there would be a great sadness in his eyes. He had been a chef in the Messageries Maritimes, and it seemed that he knew every island and every port whose name begins with M: Madagascar, Mauritius, Mombasa, Martinique. He recalled the women coaling at Fort de France in Martinique, and the rumpus that arose when some chivalrous officials thought the work unseemly for them. Not a bit of it: with their loins tightly girt by an extra strip of cotton they could do the work as well as any men. And three days of it enabled them to spend the rest of the week idle in the country. Black as the burden on their heads, and as regularly spaced as the buckets on a dredger, this endless chain of women carried their laden baskets aboard by one gangway, returning ashore with them empty by another.

Monsieur Chrétien remembered, too, the many beggars who claimed to be the sole survivor of the Mont Pelé eruption in 1902—the criminal who, being in the condemned cell, deep underground, had escaped the burning ashes. Strange that one man condemned to death by his fellows should be the one man to survive them in the disaster. Monsieur Chrétien shook his head slowly—the machinations of fate were beyond his comprehension.

And while we were talking of the scalding waters that pour their way down the bare volcanic slopes of Mont Pelé, we could hear the cool green waters of the Seine tumbling over the mill weir by the bridge. I made a drawing of the wheel-house a few days after my arrival. It pleased everyone in the village, especially the miller. "Ce n'est pas une impression," he said, "c'est la vérité." He insisted on my showing it at the café on the other side of the bridge, and I had begun to explain that it was not meant to be anything more than an illustration in a book descriptive of the Seine when there was a general outburst of opinion among the company. Why certainly, they said, if you are writing of the country that is not known to others, you must make the drawings very clear for them to understand. It is different if you are making decorations for a poem of which all know the subject: then it is correct that your drawing should find only the music of the poem. One of them mentioned Mallarmé. "The substance of his poems is very small, it is the colour of his words that matter. A suitable drawing must be like another piece of music—a variation of the same theme, played on a different instrument." One would be surprised to hear such conversations from rustics in a wayside pub in England; in France it became no surprise to me at all, even in the smallest buvette. After that evening I noticed that the prices of my drinks in the café were reduced by ten per cent.

Madame, at the hotel, as gay in her movements as her husband was stately, carried dishes to the dining-room or glasses to the long room behind the kitchen where villagers relaxed their minds with cards and dice, and refreshed their bodies with red or white wine, with a *pernod* or a beer. Her husband said to me one day: "I wish you would teach my wife to speak English. The English visitors come here, they say my omelette aux champignons is love-lee; they say my bifsteck is love-lee; they say my wife is love-lee. What do they mean by that word?"

One day in the long room a farmer spoke to me. He said that he occupied himself with the *élevage* of chickens, and that he was a *libre penseur*. Had I read anything of Anatole France? he asked. I mentioned *Penguin Island*. "Ah, *L'Île des Pingouins*!" he exclaimed. "Le sommet de la littérature française! Chaque mot juste comme le knock-out d'un

boxeur." If I hadn't moved quickly I'd have had a demonstration on the point of my chin. He told me that he was forty-three and that he had never told a lie to his wife, that she was "la meilleure opération de ma vie." Only the day before in the hotel I had heard a Dutchman, equally loving but tired of being kept waiting, refer to his wife as "my sweet disaster."

My new friend, the elevator of chickens, invited me to his house. It had been, he told me, "le rendez-vous de chasse des Comtes de Tavannes." It was the house with the tower on the other side of the bridge, beside the café in fact. Why not go with him now?

The main entrance seemed out of repair, so he took me to a doorway in the tower and thence by a spiral stone staircase into a large room on the first floor. It was richly panelled in oak, with a magnificent stone fire-place at one end and at the other a huge cupboard decorated with emblems of the chase. But from end to end of the room, just clear of the fire-place and the cupboard, was a high fence of lattice wire, and behind the wire were about a hundred and fifty white pullets—"Wee-an-dotes," he called them. Then he led me into the next room, his library. There wasn't even a cupboard here, nothing but shelves of books and dust. A brush and a duster had to be found before a book could be opened. But here were his special editions of Anatole France, and with them a copy of *Salammbô*. He didn't really think much of Flaubert, he told me. *Salammbô* was certainly a tour de force, but you could feel that it had been an effort, whereas *L'Île des Pingouins* sang with gaiety. Even so, he said, there was no denying that Flaubert's power to build up an episode such as that of the mutilated elephants was tremendous. Then he unearthed, almost literally, three paintings that had been leaning with their faces against the wall. There were two landscapes and a nude torso. The latter I liked very much and said so: it had delicate colour and sensitive modelling. I suggested that he should do more in that vein. But instead of replying he brought forward another landscape. It was no better than the other two, and when I reverted to the torso his answer was to produce yet another green field and cottage. Why did he not do more figures, I asked, adding that they were so obviously his métier. He hesitated a moment and then confessed that the torso was the only one in the collection that he hadn't painted.

These first-floor rooms into which I had been taken were on a level with the hillside at the back of the house, and from them we stepped into a yard where ducks, goats and a young bull held court. Once on a time nobles and gallant ladies on horseback, in gay attire and with pages and lackeys in attendance, had gathered here to follow hounds through the forest, questing the wild boar or the deer. Now the only one in the yard in gay attire was a bantam cock. He was the only huntsman there, too.

I have an idea that cows are treated very gently in this district. I have seen women standing among them for hours on end, quietly knitting while they watched their charges graze. One day as I sat at the river's edge, drawing, I became aware of a presence beside me. A moment later it was in front of me—a huge mouse-coloured cow, of the Châtillon breed, that came closer and closer as if to lick my face. The usual *shush* with a wave of the arm had no effect. It was only when I tapped her wet muzzle with the back of my drawing-board that she withdrew. I wonder what Gulliver's reactions would have been if he had found himself in a land where cows rather than horses held sway. Though born in Ireland I am not a horseman. My father could never afford to keep better than a broken-winded Welsh pony or one from Iceland with eczema in its tail. How often those unhealthy bristling hairs offended me as, sitting behind them in a trap, I tried to urge their owner to a trot. But we always kept two good cows. My first woodcut was of Spot, a shorthorn, and my second of a Kerry whose name I have since forgotten. She didn't mean so much to me, but then I hadn't helped her in her troubles as I had Spot. It was early one Sunday morning that Boss Payne, our "man about the place," woke me with stones against my window. "Come down, Mister Bob," he said. "Spot is bad." She was certainly in pain when I reached the cowshed, and I could do no more than I was told. I won't go into details. The calf was born by means that still seem to me incredible, and then I just had time to find the helping farmer a drink before rushing off to teach in Sunday school. There is a man alive today, a knight of the realm, a director of one of the biggest engineering concerns in the world, and to what does he attribute all his success but to my teachings in Sunday school. The fact is that all I ever taught him was to escape with me whenever we could to the bogs to find a few snipe or maybe a duck.

But to return to cows. For some reason we are apt to speak of them in derogatory phrases, yet poets write with ecstasy of the very conditions enjoyed supremely by these animals: treading the dewy grass at dawn, lying in the sun amid buttercups and daisies, standing breast-deep in the stream when the day is hot. They haven't yet celebrated the value of its tail, but that is bound to come. Now there's a perquisite that man was surely unwise to surrender. How landscape painting would flourish if by an unconscious rhythmic swishing an artist could keep at bay those hordes of insects that make havoc of his thoughts. Self-supporting, pendant yet independent, knowing its place and keeping to it, and with all the goodwill in the rump aiding the intentions of the higher centres of cerebral activity. There is a proverb, three centuries old at least, that says: "The cow knows not what her tail is worth till she hath lost it."

Our attitude to cows is not unlike our attitude to gipsies, envying them in many ways, yet in others esteeming them little. Who does not covet the freedom of those fellow humans whose creed it is "never to sleep twice in the same place, never to drink twice from the same well, never to cross the same river twice in one year." I like the story of the gipsy who on being released after a month in prison, which to him had probably been the equal of a year to another man, was in a state of utter depression. Nothing that his tribe could do to cheer him had any effect. At last he told them his trouble. "I was only there for thirty days," he said, "and then they let me out. Think of the jailer—he will be there all his life. That is what makes me sad."

# CHAPTER FOUR

WIDER, all the time growing wider. To follow a river is like watching the growth of a child: only at intervals is one conscious of the increase in its strength, from brook to brook, from weir to weir, as from week to week. Mills all the way: for grinding flour, for cutting timber, for cutting stone—scarcely a mile in which the river has not been made subject to man's needs. At one time there were paper-mills at Courceaux, only three miles from its source.

About ten miles below Aisey, at Châtillon, the Seine meets its first important confluent, the Douix, the shortest and the daintiest of all its tributaries. One hundred and twenty-five paces in length, yet as wide as the longer river at their junction. Crystal clear, it emerges full-grown from under a high limestone cliff festooned with ivy and trailing box and crested with chestnut, ash and elder. Birds flight and dip from spray to spray, their piccolo notes echoing from the rock face. Kingfishers flash blue; bullfinches whirl from bough to bough; wagtails glint yellow in parabolic flight from tree tops to the water's edge. Even in its short length the river has a bridge of its own, and from there, looking down into the water, one sees trailing fronds of weed clear and sparkling as flowers in a glass paper-weight.

One of my vices is that I am over-punctual. I hate the idea of keeping anyone waiting as much as I hate being kept waiting myself, and so from a dislike of wasting time I spend hours killing it. Thus it was that I found myself sitting in the bus shelter of the war-wrecked square of Châtillon with half an hour to spare before any sort of

conveyance would take me to the village of Mussy, a few miles further downstream. I was putting a point on a new pencil when I heard a voice addressing me in English.

"Would you be an artist?" asked a middle-aged man in rough tweeds. His voice was so soft that it seemed scarcely more than a whisper.

"I would," I said.

He paused a moment. "Would you be a writer as well?" he asked.

"I would," I said.

He smiled. "Would your name be Gibbings?"

"It would."

"I come from Ireland myself," he said.

Then he told me that he too was an artist, and that his name was O'Farrel and that he was on a sketching holiday. He'd been to Paris for a couple of days but the noise had driven him out. How could any artist work with a noise in his head like that? he asked. He himself couldn't work at all if there was one sound within his hearing. 'Twas only a short while ago, he said, that a little bird, a kind of a woodpecker, had come into his garden, and for a week he couldn't paint with the tapping. From the dawn of day to the dusk of night it went on—tap, tap, tap: it nearly drove him mad. So in the end he went to a friend of his who had a gun. "Could you give me the loan of your gun?" he asked. "I could," said his friend, "but I haven't it with me this week. Will you come in after Sunday?" 'Twas a Thursday then, and 'twas four days before Monday, and all the time the little bird kept on tapping and he couldn't put brush to paint. So on the Monday morning he put on his hat to go for the gun and he turned the handle of the lock and he opened his front door, and just as he was going out of the door didn't he think of St. Francis. "What would he have done? I thought. So I didn't go out of the door, and I put my hat back on the rack and I went upstairs again and I took up my palette, and do you know I didn't hear the little bird any more."

My bus came in and I said good-bye. O'Farrel was waiting for one that would take him to Auxerre where St. Patrick had been ordained. It was a pilgrimage any Irishman ought to make, he said. He would visit the cathedral and perhaps do some sketching on the Yonne.

I was glad to leave Châtillon. It is a sad town, hardly more than a crater rim of ancient houses surrounding its burnt-out core. In 1940 the inhabitants, warned of impending bombardment by the Italians, fled to the fields. There was none to check the flames.

The seats in French autocars are never very large; those in the car to Mussy seemed exceptionally small. A big roistering man in blue cotton jacket and trousers squeezed in beside me. He was talking when he got into the bus and he never stopped talking the whole seven miles to Gommeville, and because his words came so fast and because of the noise of the bus I hardly understood a word of what he said. At Gommeville where he alighted I got out also, for the joints in my legs were cracking and it was only another mile or so to Mussy. We went into the local buvette together, and there I apologized to him for my lack of comprehension. Then he spoke to me very slowly. Words were not necessary, he said: it was the face that spoke. He had been a prisoner of war for years in Germany, and he had met many prisoners of other peoples—Czechs, Americans, English, Russians. They could not speak his language but he could understand them by their faces. "If the face is good the words are good." He asked me where I came from and I told him. "Ah, l'Irlande," he said, "a country of laughing people and crying songs."

At Gommeville the water-power grinds wheat, at Mussy it crushes mustard seed. Hard as metal and small as pinheads, the mustard seeds are soaked before being tipped into the churn-like mill. As grape-shot they enter the mill, as a viscous yellow paste they emerge. Already the air is tinged with a familiar pungency. Into another mill and yet another goes that paste, emerging each time brighter in colour and finer in texture until like molten gold it oozes its stately way into great vats, there to be seasoned with vinegar; from the vats into bottles or stone jars, and thence to the platters. In the Dijon district white wine is preferred to vinegar.

I had hoped to make a drawing of the several weirs at Mussy and the lace-like frou-frou of their waters; but I had scarcely exchanged the aroma of mustard for the fragrance of a canal when the surface of the water was broken by heavy drops of rain, as if by the rising of a multitude of fishes. An hour later, clear waters were being sullied by the scourings of the streets and the sky was grey as flint. Yet another hour and no hope remained of better weather. There was a bus going to Troyes and I found a seat in it. But I saw nothing of the country: a downpour had commenced that didn't stop for days, and nothing but spectral tree along the road and ghost-like houses in the villages were visible through the streaming distorted windows. The weather had been bad while I was at Dijon and Beaune, and I had met rain like this a few times on my journey, but generally of shorter duration and at night. It hadn't interfered greatly with my travels. I had little idea what the present deluge was preparing for me.

# *CHAPTER FIVE*

TROYES is an ancient and historic town. It knew the tread of Attila's hordes. Joan of Arc, having driven the English and their allies the Burgundians from its walls, set up her banners there. Nine years earlier, in 1420, the Treaty of Troyes had been signed by which Henry V of England was granted the hand of Katherine of France in marriage, and with it the regency of the kingdom. It was in French opinion "un abominable traité," the insane King of France, Charles VI, being persuaded to it by his wife Isabeau of Bavaria, "une étrangère sensuelle et dangereuse," who had designs of her own for a country torn by civil war. Henry died two years later, within a few months of his father-in-law and before he had been crowned King of France. The sacred oil which had been brought by a dove direct from heaven for the anointing of Clovis, the first Christian king of the Franks, and which had been used (without loss of volume) at the anointing of Charlemagne and St. Louis and at many other coronations, never touched his head. There were some, therefore, who believed that Henry could not rightly be considered a king.

During the Middle Ages the great fairs of Troyes attracted merchants from all over Europe and from many parts of Asia: a number of the street names bear witness to those activities—Rue des Changes, Rue du Marché aux Noix, Rue du Marché au Pain. Streets are narrow, houses are rickety; but for their framework of timber they must surely have crumbled. In the Rue des Chats, which might be translated "Cats Alley," the leaning walls touch at their gable ends. It has been said of the houses

that they are as unlike each other as a chance gathering of human beings: Some are tall, others short; some are slight, others stout; some are straight, others are bent under the weight of years. And churches—the town is full of them: the cathedral of SS. Peter and Paul, the church of

Ste. Madeleine, the church of St. Urbain, the churches of St. Remi, St. Vizier, St. Jean, St. Pantaléon, St. Nicolas. "Yes," said a bookseller to me as I bought a map of the district, "we have many great churches in Troyes."

"And you are all much the better for them?" I asked.

"Oh yes," he said. "They are very good for *le tourisme*."

It was in Troyes towards the end of the twelfth century that there was born to a shoemaker named Pantaléon a son whom he christened Jacques, a son who in 1261 at St. Peter's in Rome was consecrated pope, taking the name of Urbain IV. A year later, on the site of his father's workshop, that same pope began the building of a church which he dedicated to St. Urbain, the first pope of that name. It has been called a gem of pure Gothic. It certainly seemed to me the loveliest of all the churches of Troyes; so comely are its forms that one would have expected it to be dedicated to a female saint, so delicate is the tracery of its pillars, buttresses and windows that one would fear for it in a storm. The skill of human hands has not obscured the purpose of the work: the carvers and masons have abstained from exploiting God to display their own accomplishment.

In the year 1516 the Grand Vicars of the church at Troyes pronounced sentence against certain insects that were damaging the vines, threatening them with excommunication if they did not disappear within six days. Counsel was appointed for the accused and a prosecutor appeared for the vine owners. The proceedings were, of course, legal because "all beasts being subject to man are therefore subject to Church Law." Ten years later the same authority proclaimed that "caterpillars, palmer-worms, or by whatever name they may be called" were banished from the diocese of Troyes. These were but two of many similar proceedings of that time. On 17th August 1487, the Cardinal Bishop of Autun, a town about a hundred miles south of Troyes, hearing that slugs were devastating the country, ordered public processions in every parish, and enjoined upon the slugs to quit the territory within three days or take the consequences and be accursed. It was emphasized to the congregation at the same time that a prompt payment of tithes would help considerably in the efficacy of the anathema.

But it wasn't only in the Middle Ages that conjuration proved effective against pests. Thanks to the American Folk Lore Society, I am able to quote from a letter written in 1948 by Miss Constance Abbott of Andover, Mass. In it she tells of how, when she was a child, her grandfather's cellar became overrun with rats, and because she was very fond of the old man she was anxious to help him. One day she read in a magazine that, merely by sending them a polite letter, rats had been induced to leave a house. She did not mention the subject to her father who "was not to be trusted with high thoughts," but occasion arose when talking with "a Mr. James White, a country gentleman of fine old family," to speak of what she had read in the magazine and to ask him what he thought of it. "He said it was true, as he knew, having himself written a letter to rats in his house, asking them to go to neighbour Sam Barnes; and sure enough next time he was over at Sam Barnes's cow-barn talking to him, Sam Barnes up and said his two barns were overrun with rats all at once and he couldn't think why." Then Miss Abbott knew that what she had read was true, and she felt it her duty to help her grandfather. "So saying nothing to nobody, I got my best writing-paper... and I wrote (and copied it nicely in ink) to the King of the Rats, in polite and complimentary terms, suggesting that we were only plain people and they must be tired of our dull food, and might like better at the home of Mr. and Mrs. George H., next house but one, because they were society people of French descent, and no doubt had choice viands." Then, telling no one, she went to her grandfather's cellar, and there she pushed the rolled-up letter "gently but firmly into the largest rat hole." Time passed, while Mr. and Mrs. H. and their three children were on holiday. But on their return, "O my! the house was full of rats who had eaten the dry groceries and of all things—wasn't it dreadful! they ate completely the face of the lovely wax doll Pauline's aunt had brought her from Paris, France, would you believe it!... Of course I did love my grandfather, and I did want to get rid of the rats, and furthermore we never did like Pauline very well, but 'Honestly God, I really didn't mean for them to eat Pauline's doll, and I never did ask them to, or know they would,' said I to Heaven."

In the town of Troyes today the most noticeable swarms of living creatures are human beings on bicycles. "It is the city with the most bicycles in all France," I was told. Everywhere in the streets one sees them, of the brightest colours—turquoise, emerald, lemon yellow, scarlet, purple—and on them young folk and old folk from every section of the community. Girls sit upright on roadsters, their rainbow skirts billowing around them; others are bent forward on racing machines, their skin-tight shorts not at all disguising the contours of their pert little posteriors. Workmen with bronzed arms, in white singlets and blue cotton trousers; pale-faced priests in dark soutanes and berets; nuns in black robes, with white, flower-like head-dresses. At the crossroads, directed by the *agent de circulation*, they all move together with the unanimity of a flock of birds or a shoal of fish.

Though kindly and hospitable, the people of Troyes have a tendency to be absent-minded. At one emporium where I bought a tent and some other camping gear, the woman of the house, wishing to add a small present for luck, offered me a jar of shaving-cream, regardless of my beard. At a café the *patron* when offering me a newspaper, offered also his spectacles, not noticing that my own were on my nose.

At that same café, one evening after dinner, a woman spoke to me. Thirty years of age, perhaps, and neatly dressed, with dark dreamy eyes and a wealth of black hair drawn into a glossy coil low on the back of her neck. She apologized for addressing me, adding that she had noticed me at the café once or twice before, and that earlier in the day she had seen me drawing in the Rue des Chats. She said that she was an artist herself, and she produced a drawing from her handbag to show me. It was made on the back of an envelope and as far as I was concerned was quite incomprehensible. She told me that she was also a poet but had forgotten to bring her poems: she had a bad memory. Then we talked of the local hero, Chrétien de Troyes, the poet who first put into writing the adventures of Sir Launcelot, Sir Perceval, and other Knights of the Round Table, the poet, indeed, who first made a literary reality of the Court of King Arthur. She declared that the English poets Malory and Tennyson owed a heavy debt to this citizen of Troyes. I said I didn't think much of all the romantic nonsense attributed to that court, that knights should have found better employment than doing silly things to please petulant females. She said that, for her, love was entirely a matter of the intellect, *cérébral.* I didn't interrupt. The story of Sir Launcelot, she continued, might never have been written had it not been for a woman, Marie de Champagne, wife of Henri I. It was her love of chivalry and romance that made her court an inspiration to the poets of her day, and it was she who not only commanded Chrétien to write the poem but from her knowledge of the Provençal Troubadours and their songs supplied him with the theme and many of its incidents. I didn't know enough then to point out that some of the incidents supplied, such as that of the hero being made to drive in a gallows-wagon, were apparently so distasteful to Chrétien that, as he tells us himself, he did not finish the poem but "gladly" handed it over to another.

As the evening wore on my companion became dreamier. She complained that the coffee was poor and not to her liking. She suggested that we should move to her *appartement* near by, where she would brew some real Mocha coffee, and then she would read me some of her poems. I tried to excuse myself by saying that I was meeting a friend, but my words sounded hollow and I don't think she believed me. God knows, there was little enough reason why she should. Half an hour later, as I paid the bill and we got up to go, I wondered how Chrétien would have extricated himself.

When we turned out of the Place into the narrow Rue Champeaux she took my arm, and it occurred to me that she was pressing it. Absent-minded or *cérébral*? I wondered. "Yes," she said, as if picking up her thoughts from earlier in the evening, "the highest love is of the brain, physical love can only be annihilating." I wished she wouldn't lean so heavily on my arm. With thunder in the air, the night was oppressive. "The mind grows richer on love, the body poorer," she said.

I tried to disengage as we crossed a narrow ill-lit alley, but absent-mindedly she kept her grip. "Yes," she mused, "to annihilate." *Écraser* was her word—it also means to bruise, to overwhelm, to ruin.

And just then a man coming from behind me caught my other arm.

Destroyed! I said to myself, and already I saw my corpse in the gutter.

"Would you be free in the morning?" asked the soft voice of O'Farrel.

My thoughts leapt from the dirty trickle of water wherein my body had almost lain. "I'm free *now*," I said.

The lady did not understand English. This was my brother, I explained, my younger beau-frère for whom I had been waiting all the evening.

Apparently cerebral activity *à trois* did not fit in with her pattern of aesthetics. She let go my arm, gave a limp finger-tip of a handshake, and disappeared into the darkness. O'Farrel and I retraced our steps to the square.

"Where did you drop from?" I asked.

"Vezelay," he said. "That church would knock you speechless. Twelfth-century Romanesque—never saw such carvings in my life. Tell me, was I wrong to follow you in the street? When I seen you in the café 'twas the way I was boiling over to have a word."

"You did me a mighty good turn," I told him.

"I only arrived an hour back," he said. "I came in by bus. But why aren't you on the river? I never thought to see you here."

"My boat is lost on the railway," I told him. "It was on its way from Tours, from Monsieur Fumard who built it for me. Maybe 'twill arrive tomorrow."

"'Tis a pity for you with the weather turned fine. Wasn't the rain last week a fright?"

"And where are you off to next?" I inquired.

"Paris in the morning," he said, "and then home. But do you know, I think I'll hold on here till the afternoon—maybe the boat will arrive in the morning and I could give you a push off on the river for luck."

# CHAPTER SIX

O'FARREL had prophesied well. Next morning as we were having coffee together, and he was again enthusing about the sculptures at Vezelay and how they obliterated the memory of everything he had seen at Auxerre, where they didn't have even a window to St. Patrick, a message was brought to me that my boat had arrived and was waiting for me in the station yard.

"My God! She's no more than a coracle," said O'Farrel when at last we found a speck of blue matchwood lying amid an agglomeration of railway trucks.

A deputy from the Touring Club de France was with us. He measured the boat: "Trois mètres cinquante," he said. That would not be difficult to transport. He would find a lorry; he would meet us after déjeuner. He agreed that even with so small a boat I had been wise not to attempt navigation above Troyes; indeed, he would instruct the chauffeur to take us a few kilometres below the town before attempting to launch.

Two hours later O'Farrel and I squeezed ourselves on to the front seat of the lorry alongside the driver. The boat and my camping gear had been hoisted in astern. "Vogue la galère!" called our friend as we waved him au revoir: "Good speed to the galley!"

Barbarey was our destination, a village about a mile and a half from the town. There we drove down a rough track to the lock. Below the weir was a boiling maelstrom of discoloured water; beyond, the river spread through the reeds and undergrowth, and lipped the edge of the road. There was no sign of either bank. The lorry-driver inquired if I could swim.

"We'll be calling you Captain Webb after this," said O'Farrel.

The little boat sat nicely on the water. To save storage space on board we shared a bottle of the red wine that I had brought with me. I thought that O'Farrel looked troubled as we said good-bye. The driver wished me "bonne chance," but there didn't seem much confidence in his voice. The two of them were still watching when, after manoeuvring under the trunk of a fallen poplar, I lost sight of them behind its branches.

My boat, eleven feet six inches in length and flat-bottomed, was indeed hardly more than a coracle, and I soon found that she had as little idea of keeping a straight course as any of her forbears of lath and hide. In calm water a stroke from either oar would swing her in a complete circle: in rough water it needed no small ingenuity, with both oars, to circumvent her eccentricities. If left to herself on the stream she would perform all the gyrations and evolutions of a floating leaf; at one moment, in an eddy pirouetting on her own axis, at the next, with the current rushing under the deepest and darkest canopies of overhanging foliage. And where the current sluiced through a labyrinth of fallen trees, the uglier the stub that reared its head above the surface the greater for her its attraction.

The current seemed inevitably to choose the most unnavigable route. Where of nature's necessity there were sudden bends I could understand its scourings from side to side; but it was beyond my comprehension why, when a long straight course lay open, it needed the most wanton divagations to satisfy its frenzy.

In a few words, how I escaped destruction once in every half-hour that day it is hard to say. Again and again it seemed that "my future was behind me." The first moment that I felt safe was after I had moored for the night in the lee of a bridge. Then, rocked gently in the arms of

Sequana, I forgot the knives she had tried to stick in my ribs during the day, I forgot the snares and deceptions she had set for me, I forgot her threats for the morrow, and when darkness fell I slept peacefully in the crook of her arm. If some eddy of the current gave a tug at the mooring rope to disturb my slumbers, it was only as though the goddess had stirred in her sleep.

Ford Madox Hueffer wrote a poem which he called *Heaven*. In it he told how he had waited in a little town in the south of France, knowing nothing of passing time, until when the years were over the woman for whom he had waited came to him, and their days together began. It was strange for her, he said, to come from England straight into heaven. "And all night long she lay in the crook of my arm"—a pretty thought and one that has often recurred to me. Alas, I snore: the crook of my arm holds no attraction. Isn't it an odd thing that he who designed marriage also designed snoring? In parts of America such nocturnal cadences are considered justification for divorce. Medical science, it seems, can do next to nothing to help. It merely tells us that "the sounds in the stertorous inhalations of the habitual snorer are produced by the vibrations of the soft tissues of the nasopharynx and oropharynx," and that the quality of those vibrations is "to some extent dependent on the tone of the musculature of the glossopharyngeal arch." But what sleep-seeking Dulcinea is going to accept those explanations at three o'clock in the morning?

My second day on the river followed much the same pattern as the first, with the face of destruction oft-times leering at me. There was no abatement in the flood. Unless resting a moment in some backwater, I dared not take my hands from the oars.

The country beside those upper reaches of the Seine is heavily timbered with poplars—great plantations of them, immensely tall and straight, in long lines. Here and there were patches where trees had been cleared and saplings planted: they were at times the only open country in what seemed a vast primeval forest, a forest whose dark vaults soared high from the depths of their own reflections. Surging water everywhere. No sound or sign of human activity. Only once in the first fifteen miles did I see solid ground. The river banks were entirely covered: it was often difficult to tell which was river and which was flood. Large yellow slugs crawled up the tree trunks to escape destruction, innumerable snails girdled the trees at water level. No cheering sound of bird song, only the raucous notes of the grey shrike to goad me on. In the dark jungle water, sodden logs lay still and slimy as crocodiles. Bare branches gesticulated, their submerged stems caught in the current.

As I was carried along on this impetuous surge, I thought of the Samoan theological student who inquired of his teacher, "Is there any easy way to keep the Ten Commandments?" Was there any way at all, I wondered, by which I might keep to the main stream? The waters raged where they listed through thickets and forests, and my course seemed beset with as many snares, delusions and treacherous beguilements as the most zealous would-be cleric could fear. It was another pupil at the same seminary who inquired: "What would the world be like if Adam and Eve had not sinned?" I wondered what my world would be like if there hadn't been this flood. Yet a third student had asked, "Why do boys wish earnestly for girls?" At that moment in my life I wished only for a steadying influence.

"Floods, floods! They kind of gits on yer nerves," a farmer in the Thames valley once said to me, after his cattle had been several times marooned.

"They fair gets on my garden," said a neighbour of his: "carried away three lines o' cabbages and a 'ole load o' manure last week."

"Worth ten quid a time to me, with the gravel they bring down," said another whose holding lay by a bend of the river.

This flood was certainly altering the land beside the Seine. Banks were being eroded and silt spread over many acres. Fallen trees were trapping floating vegetation, and then, weir-like, were thrusting currents into new channels.

I can't say that I enjoyed those first days on the water. Trees sprawled from bank to bank; it was difficult to avoid the fate of Absalom. I had no anchor to slow my course: experts at Troyes had laughed at the idea of such a thing being necessary. They forgot that this was the highest flood "since the Creation of the world." It was higher than the one in 1910 and that had exceeded all earlier records. And so I whirled and swirled along at the mercy of this goddess to whom the Romans had offered oblations for the cure of their afflictions. Was she seeking a new client in me? I wondered.

Bridges, being for the most part temporary constructions replacing those destroyed in the war, were low, and the river being high there was often little if any distance between framework and water. At one of them, where I miscalculated the clearance, my head was caught between an iron girder and the gunwale of the boat. The whole force of the flood pressed on the boat and it became a question of which would go first, my skull or the gunwale. My brain must have been nearly flat when a report as of a sixteen-inch howitzer went through it from ear to ear. Which of us has gone? I wondered. But Irish limestone builds good bone, and the cranium had won the day. At another bridge, a wooden one, just as I had abandoned myself and the boat to the current, I saw two long iron spikes protruding downwards from the timbers, ready to disembowel me. Prostrate in the boat, my stomach went flatter than it had been for many a day, and I lost no more than a button.

But between these times of torment there were moments when it was possible to manoeuvre the boat over calm meadows and there to swim, looking down on submerged grasses as though they were soft corals gently swaying on a tropic reef. Away from the chilly aisles of trees the sun shone warm, and the ocean of dark threatening waters became a fairy world of shining glass. Floating over it I would see field paths and cattle tracks, and once an iron plough reminded me of Tir na n-Og and other islands drowned by enchantment.

In the first days of my journey it was only at bridges that I made any contact with other human beings; it was, indeed, only at bridges that I saw dry land. At the first one of all, less than a mile from Troyes, the arches were so completely filled with water that most of the river was going over the road on one side, a course that I too followed in my boat. I spoke to an old woman whose cottage adjoined the road and who was looking ruefully at what remained of her garden above the flood line. "You will be drowned," was her only comment when I said I was on my way to Paris. More cheerful were two young men in rubber thigh-boots who appeared at a bridge a little lower down, just when I saw no possibility of getting my craft either under or over the obstruction. It was no trouble to them, they said, they were accustomed to boats, they were accustomed to rivers and obstructions. I gathered that they were also accustomed to poaching. They said there were some big trout in the pool below the bridge. They had come to see the state of the water, but it was still too high for business. "Mais certainement," at any time of the year a throw-net was illegal. Then as if jealous for their river's honour: "You must not write about it as it is now," they said. "That would not be fair. Where there are three metres of water today you can walk across with dry feet in other years." Then we talked about dogs. Yes, they knew the red "setter Irlandais," knew it well: a fine dog, but not much good in this country where it was too marshy for anything but duck. Had I seen many duck?

"Thousands," I answered, and I spoke without exaggeration, for time and again in the denser parts of the forest flocks of fifty or a hundred or more of them had startled the life out of me as they rose splashing and squawking from the reeds. The boys said that there were few snipe in those parts but plenty of woodcock. I looked up as a heron passed overhead. "Un grand pêcheur," one of them commented, "beaucoup de poissons dans son ventre."

Clouds were banking in the western sky, tall towering clouds that so often portend a storm. The horizon below them was red as copper. Half an hour later it was as though the distant countryside was in flames. My friends had left me—one might expect "un petit orage", they said—and I was pitching my tent on the dry slope between bridge and flood when distant rumblings caught my ear. As I looked up, two molten bars of light connected the heavens and the earth. A minute later the rain on the wooden bridge sounded like the pattering of sheep's hoofs. Soon, as I lay in the tent, I could hear trickles on the slope beside me. I wondered how soon they would find their way into the tent. And then, as suddenly as it had begun, the rain ceased. The storm passed all round but did not come overhead. At dawn the sky was clear and the air sparkling.

The roads on either side of the bridges were generally under water, but one morning near Savières I found a dry path that led to the village. There I purchased provisions, and having returned to the boat set off again. The river twisted and turned through kilometre after kilometre of sodden wilderness. Tree after tree lay across my course. One of them nearly blinded me with a springing branch; another did its best to comb me out of the boat. There was I, hanging among the branches, my feet only on the inner side of the gunwale, and the water a cataract below me. Fortunately the boat stuck in a fork of the tree, and with a sudden gift of agility I regained my place on the thwart.

Many a time that day I had to diverge from the actual river and seek my way across flooded acres, hostile with bramble, nettles and thistles; many a time, too, I thought that Sequana was luring me to follow streams that dissipated themselves in a welter of thorn and thicket, and against whose current it would have been impossible to return.

It was late in the afternoon when I came to the next bridge, and the first piece of high land that I had seen on my journey. There was a house there, too, inhabited by a kindly old man from the Vosges. He directed me to the village, its war memorial and its buvette. From the river, throughout the day, there hadn't been a yard of cultivated land to be seen, not a house nor an animal nor a man in sight; yet when I had walked a few hundred yards up the track I found rich open country, a main road running between fields of wheat and oats and a village whose inhabitants seemed as oblivious of the secret world of water and swift currents hidden among the trees as I had been of any other world throughout the day. It was even more of a surprise to me to see on a signboard the name of the village—Savières, the very place from which I had set out long hours before. The river has many *boucles*, they told me, and the village is long and straight. But, fortunately, the buvette stood where I had seen it in the morning.

# CHAPTER SEVEN

ON the table of the café at Savières was an ash-tray bearing the inscription: "Mon petit ventre console-toi, tout ce que je bois c'est pour toi," which being interpreted means "My little belly, console yourself, all that I drink is for you alone." And on the counter of the same bar was another which said: "Quand ton verre est plein, vide-le; quand il est vide, plains-le" ("When your glass is full, empty it; when it is empty, pity it").

They have a liking for such ash-trays in France. Piquant and worldly wise, one finds them almost everywhere, in cafés and restaurants and often in private houses. "Love makes time pass, time makes love pass"; "One is always twenty years of age in some corner of the heart"; "There are no lost women: they always find themselves again"; "Don't make love on a Saturday afternoon or you'll have nothing to do all Sunday." In a village in Burgundy, appropriately enough, I saw "The key to Paradise may be found in the cellar."

That evening at Savières I remarked to a man in the café that the subjects of these inscriptions seemed somewhat restricted. He said: "En France il y a quatre choses élémentaires: bien manger, bien boire, bien baiser, bien dormir. Après, fini."

Stars were in the sky as I made my way back to the boat. I overtook an old man who, with a spade over his shoulder, had stepped on to the road from a field ahead of me. "You are working late!" I remarked to him.

He looked at me as if in surprise. "Il faut travailler jusqu'à la mort," he said.

We walked a short way together, and I told him of my journey on the river and that I had been hoping the floods would have gone down more quickly. He made no comment at first; we had reached a cottage set back a little from the road, and he had stopped to open the gate. It was after he had gone through and latched it behind him that he turned and looked at me sadly. "In life one should never hope," he said.

There was no light that I could see in the house. I supposed that he must live alone.

That night I slept ashore *à la belle étoile*—no need for a tent. My only regret as I lay down was the crushing of the grass—sad that you cannot take one step in a meadow without bruising some live thing. I remembered reading somewhere that there is a bigger population of living organisms in a piece of soil that would fit on a shilling than there is of people in one of the larger countries of Europe. In the cities life is an expenditure of capital energy, self-consuming; pavements are sterile, death is the end. But in the country even death begets life. Everything alive or "dead" throbs with vitality; to touch anything is to partake of its *mana*.

Dreams, nervous twitchings of the mind, did not trouble me that night. I woke early, ready to continue the battle. Birds were greeting the day; the air was like silk. But the river looked fierce as ever. My host from the Vosges tried to encourage me by saying that its level had dropped several centimetres during the night—as well talk of pints at Niagara. Again there were prostrate trees to negotiate, submerged stumps to avoid, often with scarcely a herringbone ripple to betray them. There were echoes of falling waters to mislead, sudden splashings of rising ducks to startle, raucous cries of shrikes to jeer, and herons with their supercilious flight to mock. When, lost in the disorder of quarrelling streams, I found myself in a featureless forest, a shadow from a cloud, silent as a cat's step, would deepen what was already gloom. I would hardly have been surprised if an arrow had whizzed past my head and long-haired, befeathered American Indians in dug-out canoes had assailed me. I would hardly have been surprised if some trailing branch had resolved itself into a constrictor snake, or if a host of chattering monkeys had swung through the boughs above me. And then, as though my oars had been magic wands, three strokes would take me into quiet water and serene sunshine. "Strip off and enjoy yourself," I'd say to myself, "for the one thing you're sure of is NOW."

Isn't the sun on one's body marvellous? The best tonic in the world. Why, even a blade of grass grows pale for the want of it. A very rich man I once knew kept pedigree cows as a hobby. He wasn't satisfied that they should live in the fields and come to the stalls only for milking; it was too rough a life for them, he thought, insanitary and weakening their resistance to infection. So he built houses for them with every modern convenience that a cow could desire—wash-hoof basins and all the rest—and there the cows resided, being taken for a walk in the fields morning and afternoon by highly sanitated herdsmen or was it herdsgirls, I can't remember. And then an inspector came along and said the milk of the cows was lacking in all the vitamins that mattered and

that it must not be sold to the public. So the owner disposed of the whole herd to his neighbour, a farmer, who turned them out into the meadows day in, day out, and shortly reaped a fortune from the quality of their milk. Meanwhile my friend turned his attention to Art and, having a more natural understanding of pigments and clay than of udders and mud, he bought wisely, sold astutely and recovered from the studios what he had lost in the cowsheds.

Two miles downstream, as I approached St. Mesmins, I saw women scrubbing clothes in a backwater on the left bank. Ahead of me I could hear the river thundering through sluice-gates. Was there any way of circumventing the weir? I inquired. No, there was no way round. "But," said a young and powerful woman, "the little barque is not heavy, one can carry it." She rose from her kneeling board and came to the water's edge. It was only a matter of pulling it up the hill into the village and then down again on the other side of the mill, she explained. She took hold of the bow as if to do so, but the barque was heavier than she had expected. "Ça ne fait rien," she would get help. Off she went, to return a few minutes later with a brawny man stripped to the waist and covered with flour. Another from the bakery followed, bringing a small trolley, and in no time at all the boat was on wheels. But all too soon one of the wheels had fallen off and she was aground in mid village. That didn't seem to matter either. By now every local inhabitant including the curé and the gendarme had begun to take an interest and give advice. Young men brought rollers, old women pushed, children pulled: the boat went up the hill as fast as ever it had come through the eye of a bridge. Through the village square and into the water on the other side, with an ever increasing crowd to admire *la jolie petite barque bleue*. No, not one of them would take a franc. "C'est un plaisir, monsieur," they said, or "À votre service, monsieur." Nowhere in the world have I met greater willingness to help than in those upper reaches of the Seine. Whatever daft request I might make—and many of them must have seemed daft—the answer was invariably: "Mais comme vous voudrez, monsieur." It is true that sometimes they would tell me what they thought I wished to hear: distances would become shortened, difficulties lessened, sometimes even weirs and bridges removed; but then I've known as much to happen elsewhere. At Vallant St. Georges, a further two miles on my way, I met similar treatment. Here the wooden bridge was so low that there was scarcely daylight to be seen between its beams and the flow of the river. Once again it was necessary to lift the boat, and once again as if from nowhere men appeared, carrying hammers and a crowbar. They had come to repair a fault in the bridge, but they saw no reason why they shouldn't add another fault or two if it would ease the passage of the boat. By knocking off a few side rails she went over with scarcely an effort on my part. "Bon voyage," they called, as once again the current strove for mastery.

*Bon voyage* indeed! They had warned me that I must be careful at the *barrage,* the weir, that I would meet about two kilometres downstream. The current there was swift and dangerous, they said. They did not know whether I should keep to the right or the left bank—with the flood it was impossible to tell. I must go slowly and inquire before getting too close.

It wasn't long before I heard the sound of rushing water from somewhere beyond the next bend in the river. I'll do as they told me and be careful, I thought. So pulling in to the bank, I climbed ashore. The bank itself was thick with thistles, beyond it lay a swamp thick with brambles. The water in the swamp was knee deep at first and later it was above my waist, with innumerable unseen stubs of felled trees among the brambles, and in one place strands of barbed wire from a broken fence. And my only armour was my bathing-trunks. There came a time when short of being completely flayed by unseen claws I must return to the boat. But at any rate I had seen that level water still lay ahead.

I edged the boat carefully round the bend and found an even wider stretch of river than I had expected. But at the end of it, where it narrowed under a hill, there was a high iron *digue,* a sluice gate, and it was thence that the sound had come to me. I manoeuvred the boat into a quiet backwater almost hidden under trees at the foot of the rising ground, and once again clambered ashore. Here I found a track that led upwards through the undergrowth, and I hadn't climbed far before I could see the chimney of a house. That's good, I thought; I'll be able to get help or at any rate advice. Then I heard the barking of a dog. That's good too, I thought; the house is inhabited. I noticed a strange smell in the air, heavier than whitethorn and more fetid. The nearer I got to the building the stronger became the smell. The air seemed polluted. Then ahead of me the house came into full view. It was, in fact, a large barn, solitary, grim, with not a sign of life or implement about the place except the dog tugging at its chain and barking. There wasn't as much as a chicken or a duck to liven it up, there didn't seem even a sparrow to pick a straw for nest-building. As I came closer the dog began to show its teeth—wonderful how white and regular a dog's teeth can be. I became more conscious of my scanty attire and picked up a long stick that lay near the path. The dog began to bark again. Still no sign of a human being. The stench grew stronger, and now another dog appeared from its kennel on the other side of the path, and its teeth were even whiter and the scruff of its neck more bristling than those of the first. I almost laughed to think of the way I was "enjoying" myself on the river.

But why was there no humanity about the place? Perhaps they were busy inside the barn. I synchronized a wild swipe of the stick with a blind bounce of the body, and found myself beyond the two dogs and in front of the wide-open doors. Then I looked inside. There, for all to see and admire, were the bodies of two large horses, suspended from the rafters by great iron hooks, with their bellies open and their entrails spread about the floor. And there was I, naked beside them, with a Cerberus on every side, for two more hideous brutes were now out of their kennels ahead of me. There is a theory that a realization of self in relation to one's surroundings at any particular moment greatly increases the appreciation of that moment. I had no need of any esoteric instruction just then. I was very much aware of every twisted, contorted form before me; I sensed the livid entrails beside the sleek coats of the victims; I saw the gleam of four straining chains; I saw the snarling teeth of four infuriated beasts, and I saw my own naked skin. Strangely enough I felt little apprehension: it was like some nightmare from which, unlike nightmares, I was assured of waking up.

I won't continue. I give my fair and honest word that what I have told is an understatement. Eventually in a field far removed from this idyll of Poe or Dante I found a ploughman. He said that the *digue* above which I had anchored was of little importance, merely controlling a canal, that the true course of the river swung in the other direction, and that in it there was a concrete *barrage* which was quite impassable. He added that one couldn't possibly carry the boat overland on this side of the river, and suggested that I should row upstream, cross over to the other bank, and there find help. He also showed me a less embarrassing route back to the boat.

And here is the anticlimax. When I did row upstream, when I did cross over to the other side, but before I had sought further aid, I discovered that nothing of the *barrage* remained but one isolated lump of concrete in midstream. The flood had carried the rest of it away. I sailed through the channel as a liner might pass the Needles.

# CHAPTER EIGHT

SLEEP, deep untroubled sleep. Isn't it odd how we love oblivion? I often think that, when tossing and turning in bed, the best inducement to unconsciousness is to think of all the most comfortless places in which at one time or another we have been compelled to spend a night: wedged upright in a smoke-filled railway carriage, clinging to one's bunk during a Channel storm, herded in an air-raid shelter. Then we appreciate the uncramped luxury of a bed, and soon we are asleep. Perhaps, equally, it is good to dwell on the happiest of our drowsy moments—on a mountainside with no roof overhead but heaven and no sound in one's ears but of the wind in the grasses; or on an islet in a lake, with heaped-up rushes as a bed and hearing only the bleat of a snipe; or beside a river, under a canopy of lime-trees whose branches hum with the drone of bees. It is the mountainside that I remember from my journeying on the Wye; it is the islet that I remember from the time when I was writing *Lovely is the Lee*; it is the "bee-loud" lime-tree, that evening above the village of Méry, that I shall recall from my voyage on the Seine.

The river now had become comparatively wide: even the tallest of fallen poplars left some small channel for my boat. I moved through a majestic water-borne forest, only the wider aisle among the trees betraying the river's course. I began to hope for a less eventful journey. The hopes didn't last long. Of a sudden I found myself almost on top of yet another *barrage*, a line of sluice gates right across the river. I had barely time to hurl my rope into the branches of a drowned tree. By now there was on the end of the rope a chunk of iron which I had picked up at my last landing—I felt those dogs owed it to me. It held.

A dense wall of reeds made it almost impossible to land from the boat; it was easier to swim ashore and claw my way through that palisade. What did it matter that the land beyond was under water? I was dressed for the occasion.

Half an hour later a miller and his wife, his mother and three children, were not a little surprised to see a stranger who could only have emerged from the flood standing in their yard. Nor did they seem displeased; something really had arrived to stir the quiet of their Sunday afternoon. White rabbits in hutches, white pigeons on the roof, a white cat and a friendly black-and-white dog, all gave the scene an air of peace. Would I not have *un petit verre*? they asked after I had explained my difficulty. It was of their own make, flavoured with mirabelle.

Talk of a "torch-light procession down the throat"! The buckle on the belt of my trunks nearly melted. But wasn't it a comfort?

The miller said that under present conditions the main river was impossible for any craft, but that if I could get my boat to the other side a little higher up I would find the entrance to the mill stream. Once there I could transfer to a branch of the Seine that would take me to Sauvage, a matter of six or seven kilometres, and after that it was clear sailing to Paris.

Apart from the dog, who stayed to mind the house, the whole family, including the cat, accompanied us as the miller and I set out. The cat, finding too many puddles on the track, came but a short distance, and perhaps for the same reason the grandmother and youngest child soon followed its example and left us. There came a point when even the miller could come no further for want of waders. But he had been able to show me where I might find the opening to his stream. He suggested that, to row against the current being almost impossible, it would be best to keep close in to the bank, and by pulling on the reeds make my way upstream as far as I could before attempting to cross.

Handfuls of reeds make a poor hawser, and as I worked myself along, snatching at the greener stems for strength, I wondered just how much grip they had in the river-bed. When, all too soon, a few limp roots hung in my hand, I learnt that it was frail. Already the bow of the boat had swung into the stream and there wasn't another reed within reach. There was nothing for it but to row and row hard, with the line of sluice-gates staring me in the face like so many grinning guillotines. I reached the other side with a couple of feet to spare between me and perdition.

Well, so much for *that* little tussle. Except that it was not so wide, the stream on which I now found myself was much the same as the main river. Like everywhere else in the valley, there was "trop d'eau." The same impetuous currents rushed from side to side, the same torrents poured through broken and bending reeds, the same wastes of flood lay all around, and the river being narrower I again had difficulties with fallen trees. It was getting monotonous.

There came another night under the stars, following a three-course dinner of three boiled eggs. Was it tidiness, or was there some remnant of old superstition in my skull, that made me put my spoon through the bottom of each finished egg to make it sink? At any rate, the luck was with me next morning. I was going along smoothly and quietly enough, and had almost reached the village of Sauvage, when I heard an imperative shout from behind a screen of willow on the right bank. "Attention! Attention!" called the voice. A man was gesticulating to me to stop. I threw my rope and he pulled me ashore. Fifty yards more, he said, and I'd have been in the mill-race.

He introduced himself as Maxime Cabourdin. Tall and lean, with greying hair and fine-cut features, his manners combined the graciousness of the château with the simple directness of the cottage. He was a gardener, he told me, and he seemed delighted to put aside his work in order to help me. "À votre service, monsieur," he said. Unlike everyone else whom I had met on the river, he did not ask if I could swim; but he urged, indeed he almost commanded, that I should go no further until the flood had subsided.

"And how long will that be?" I asked.

"Eight days, perhaps two weeks."

"And what about the boat?"

"It is well here. This is my garden."

"And the blankets and the tent?"

"My wife will take care of them."

It occurred to me that a few days in Paris might be a pleasant change. I hadn't seen much vehicular traffic of late. Monsieur Cabourdin went to find a taxi that would take me to the station, while I put on some clothes.

Three hours later I was going through my mail in an armchair overlooking the Boulevard Raspail. Among some press cuttings was a particularly nice review of my book *Sweet Cork of Thee* from the *Irish Independent*, signed "N. N." It began by saying: "Mr. Gibbings is now turned sixty and ought to have sense instead of gallivanting around the queer places of the world." You're right, me boy, I said to myself, but whatever nom de plume nobility "N. N." stands for, it also stands for "now or never."

# CHAPTER NINE

JACQUELINE and Gustav, to whom with gratitude and affection I dedicate this book, were living in their flat next door to the small hotel in Montparnasse in which, all unaware of their proximity, I had spent the previous Christmas. It wasn't till the following April that the chance remark of a mutual friend with whom we had shared wartime experiences brought us together again. From that day onward the flat was as good as mine. Indeed, there were times when it was entirely mine, for they would often spend weeks in the country, leaving me in sole charge. Caviare to the sound of trumpets was Sydney Smith's idea of heaven; for myself, I would be content with Montparnasse without the screech of taxis. If the streets are not of gold they are at any rate, as Karel Capek wrote, "places where a thousandfold spectacle meets your gaze and where a thousand adventures address themselves to you." The wide terraces of the cafés are seats in the stalls, and there is a continuous performance. You can take your place at any hour of the day or night;

comedy, tragedy, romance, all are enacted before you, without pause for scene shifting.

Shops catering for the artist are thick as pubs in an Irish village, and they exhibit everything that painter, sculptor or engraver could need—nothing between them and him but a sheet of plate glass and the price label. The sight of the frames alone is enough to make a man start painting. And when brain and fingers lack harmony, there are studios where for francs the equal of a shilling you can work from a model for the whole afternoon. Drawing is like piano-playing or boxing—the physical reaction to mental stimulus must be automatic. Any consciousness of the processes involved brings failure.

"Fifty francs! I remember when it was three," I said one afternoon to Madame Rose, the *gardienne* at the Académie de la Grande Chaumière, as I paid my fee to enter.

"I remember when it was two sous," she said, smiling.

For thirty-seven years Madame Rose has been sitting there at the door of the life room, taking the entrance fees. Recently a small screen has been found to shelter her from draughts, and nowadays she wears a shawl, but otherwise she seems just as when I knew her first, more than twenty-five years ago. Every day of her life except Sundays she sits there, knitting and chatting with any models who have dropped in on the chance of a job. Art probably means little to her. All she knows of it may be that of the many who pass through the tall door of that studio only a few reach success, yet her smile is as kindly for one as for the other—for the staid old regular who hasn't missed a day in twenty years, or the youngest in his or her first eager months of training.

Attending the Grande Chaumière are many who go there day after day for years on end, for "just a little more practice." They believe that one day soon they will really begin. Their hair has whitened, their faces have aged; the only thing that hasn't altered is the standard of their work. They have become perpetual students and will remain so as long as they can hold a pencil. One finds them in every art school. They are like the young gannets who need starvation to make them take their first plunge from the nesting cliff into the sea that is to be their habitat. Not for four years will those young birds return to land: no wonder if they feel a little reluctant. The fledgling artist has no such excuse—he can always come ashore for a word of advice. Writing of such students, Robert Louis Stevenson said: "The time comes when a man should cease prelusory gymnastic, stand up, put a violence upon his will, and for better or worse, begin the business of creation. This evil day there is a tendency continually to postpone: above all with painters. They have made so many studies that it has become a habit... and death finds these aged students still busy with their hornbook."

Sitting on the semicircular benches and high stools around the model's throne are men and women of every age and every nationality. That afternoon when I dropped in, an Indian woman in olive green and crimson *sari*, her dark hair neatly coiled, sat beside a young freckle-faced girl with tousled orange hair wearing a yellow jersey and blue corduroy slacks. An elderly Frenchman with long grey beard separated a Chinaman from a middle-aged Englishwoman in homespuns. A Negress with bright head-band sat behind an ashen-blond youth with goatee beard. There were girls who might have been mistaken for boys, and boys who but for their incipient beards might well have been girls. Hairdressing has always been a subject of serious study in Montparnasse. That summer the *queue de cheval* was in favour for women—the hair drawn back and tied with a ribbon high on the back of the head so that the loose terminal swathe arched like the tail of some pretty filly. Very becoming it seemed to me, to many pretty fillies. For men, hair on the head was comparatively short, saintly unkemptness being no longer fashionable even among the most decadent. Cheeks and necks were shaved, but a thin *collier de barbe* enhanced the outline of the lower jaw.

In the studio that afternoon the model, a heavily built woman, was sitting in a huddled pose, her arms clasped around her knees. I noticed that, while the student on my right saw her as a solid sculptural mass, a pyramid with but slightly modulated surfaces, the man on my left was making a harmony of tone from the shadows on her limbs. The girl in front of me was concentrating on the outline.

It is an old story that many of the students are hard put to it to live while they study. I have seen more than one girl take a session on the model's throne; a man I know spent his non-working hours as clown in a circus. Out of the welter of it all, in each generation there emerges perhaps one artist whose name will survive.

In London spring comes to the trees and to the parks, but in Paris spring comes also to the people. "La vie de Paris qui connaît aussi le printemps." On the first warm day it would seem as if the people themselves flowered: they burst their buds and spread their coloured petals to the sun.

Sitting in the cafés, watching them pass, one realizes that much of the art which seems mannered and exaggerated is in reality simple portraiture. Until I visited Tahiti I wondered why Gauguin had distorted his women, painting them square shouldered with thick legs and large feet. But I discovered that many Tahitiennes of pure blood have those characteristics—the island film stars whom we like to gaze upon are nearly all of mixed ancestry. On the Boulevard Montparnasse one will see walking portraits of Nigerian bronzes, of Greek and Cambodian carvings. One will see profiles and draperies that can have cut themselves loose from oriental manuscripts.

One sees, too, strange witch-like women towed by their dogs from tree to tree, and men who, creating idiosyncrasies for themselves in their youth, have become slaves to them in their later years. An old man shuffles past. He is bent nearly double. Long dank wisps of hair, uncut for years, fall over his face hiding his features. His clothes are ragged, his beret dirty, but he carries a gold-mounted ebony stick and on every finger of both hands are ornate gold rings. With what ideal had he identified himself so many years ago?

Another man passes, younger but almost equally bent. He limps a little and his left hand, withered, is held behind his back. With his right hand he leads a small child, who dances by his side. She is as gay as he is sad. I wondered how a woman could have been attracted to him until I noticed the tenderness with which he treated the child.

Sooner or later one is joined by a friend or recognized by some old acquaintance. I was sitting at the Coupole one evening when a Danish painter spoke to me. He said we had met twenty years ago at the same café. He had arrived only that morning from Copenhagen, and the next day he was going into the valley of the Chevreuse to paint. Did I know of a model who would go with him? "I like to have someone to talk to at night," he said, "to take my mind off my work."

Of passers-by during the day, one in every three carries a portfolio, a paint-box or a couple of canvases. In the early morning or towards evening one in every two carries a loaf of bread also. It may be a *ficelle*, about eighteen inches in length and thin as a rope; it may be a *baguette*, more like a baton, rather stouter than a *ficelle*; or a *saucisson*, thicker still. Perhaps it is simply a *pain*, the standard loaf, about a yard in length, or a *bâtard*, a shortened variety of the same. French bread seems designed to produce the maximum of crisp crust; if it also provides a plethora of resting-places for migrant germs that matters little, for the bread is eaten so fresh that the germs have hardly got their second wind before they are digested. Baking goes on all day. Rarely can a purchaser carry home his fresh warm loaf without nibbling the end of it as he goes.

Throughout the week there are markets either on the Boulevard Edgar Quinet or on the Boulevard Raspail. Waterproof sheets over metal framework shelter the stalls. Lorries bring sacks of vegetables, crates of fruit, carcasses and cases of meat, boxes of haberdashery and suit-cases of clothes. Taxis arrive with loads of flowers. Everything is available from bust bodices and bootlaces to bluggy meat and mushrooms. In the summer of 1951, fragrant garlic tubers cost forty francs a bunch of three; carnations cost twenty-five francs a bunch of ten. Ducks and chickens, trussed and naked, are flanked by tunny fish and prawns. Frogs' legs, pale as fish flesh, twelve pairs of them in compulsory embrace on a wooden skewer for sixty francs. Slim girls in trousers, strong men wearing carpet slippers, pick and choose among the stalls. Stout old ladies in long black coats hobble under the weight of their shopping bags. On a seat apart sits a miniature man selling parsley, thyme, and other herbs at about twopence the bunch; his whole stock cannot be worth more than five shillings. Hair-nets, suspenders, boot polishes, are displayed alongside snails, sixty to a hundred francs a dozen according to size. A tall, lean man with a wooden leg demonstrates repairs to silk stockings.

On Sundays, family parties walk up and down the boulevards; husbands pushing prams or carrying infants in their arms, wives on holiday in gay attire, grandmothers in trailing black. At the corner of the Boulevards Raspail and Montparnasse throughout the year, in sunshine or in snow, artists hold informal week-end exhibitions. Each has his own gallery of canvas screens on which the paintings are hung. For the most part the work is poor, but there are always people who stop to look and presumably there are sometimes people who stop to buy.

During the days that I waited in Paris, Montparnasse was *en fête* for the Bimillénaire de Paris. The artists had got busy and every shop and café window or transparent screen glowed with the colours of stained glass. Surcouf's restaurant had, of course, a portrait and scenes from the life of Robert Surcouf, the eighteenth-century French corsair who, after a sea-going apprenticeship as slave runner between the African coast and Madagascar, became first a pirate and then a privateer, in both capacities reaping much plunder from British and Dutch shipping in the Indian ocean. Duguesclin's restaurant was no whit behind, with their namesake, a knight in armour, and other glories of medieval heraldry. The chemist's window at the corner framed a necromancer with his nightmare retorts, and a lingerie shop showed a fine frieze of silky legs. Life-size cancan dancers, reminiscent of the drawings of Toulouse Lautrec, decorated the Café du Dôme. Mandarins, staring across the Boulevard Raspail from the windowpanes of the Chinese restaurant, glimpsed a green crocodile recumbent on a couch in the pose of Manet's *Olympia*. That picture, I remembered, when first exhibited in 1863 was attacked by the academic painters as indecent, and at the artist's death twenty years later remained in his studio, unsold. Today it occupies a place of honour in the Louvre.

There had been a dance, too, a *bal costumé*. Being on the river I had missed it, but I gathered that the adjective *costumé* scarcely applied. Good fun, these student dances. You've got to be known in the quarter as an artist to gain admission; once inside it is a family affair. The models, present in force, are known to everyone and competitions for the best figure make pleasant interludes. I did not hear if on this occasion they all bathed in the fountain on their way home to breakfast, as they did when I was a boy.

# CHAPTER TEN

*Sous le pont Mirabeau coule la Seine*
*Et nos amours*
*Faut-il qu'il m'en souvienne*
*La joie venait toujours après la peine*

*Vienne la nuit sonne l'heure*
*Les jours s'en vont je demeure*

"DAYS pass and weeks go by but never past hours or loves return." With all respect and admiration I wonder why Apollinaire chose that bridge for his poem. It is an ugly metal structure with little to see from the tramlined quay under its near arch but sand heaps, gravel heaps, cranes, and accumulations of scrap-iron. Was it that he lived close by and saw it through a veil of dusk, or was there in its name the note of music that he needed? Many another work of art has been built on as flimsy a foundation.

Along the quays stretching from that Pont Mirabeau on the west of the city to the Pont d'Austerlitz a mile to the east of Notre-Dame, there is a population of *clochards*, tramps, who live a life as far removed from that of the streets above them as monks or nuns in their cloisters. "They are not *de mauvaises gens*," said an *agent de police*, "there is very seldom a dispute. It is against the law, and sometimes they must be told to move, but then they need only go to the next bridge, and they come back the next day. It is a way of life—there are people of every class who have chosen it."

I spoke to a trio of these independents, an old woman and two middle-aged men, who had pitched camp under an arch of the Pont Sully. They were sitting beside a fire on which a large saucepan of tomato soup was simmering. One of the men was breaking up a wooden fruit basket, throwing the bits of timber to the woman who added them to the fire. The other man was frying fish on a second and smaller fire. They told me that that morning, at the market, Les Halles, where they worked at night unloading produce from the country, a crate of tomatoes had fallen from one of the lorries and broken open. As the woman stirred the thick brew, other vegetables appeared at the surface. Oh yes, she laughed, accidents happened to other vegetables too. I asked the obvious question—didn't they find it cold at night? No, they said, they were used to it—anyway, the price of a room was too dear. They would rather spend their money on good food. "If you eat well, you sleep well and do not feel the cold. If you spend all your money on a room, then you have not enough for food and you are cold even under a roof." They opened a bottle of red wine and offered me the first swig.

Another family had set up house a short distance away, beneath a flight of steps. When I first saw them, a man and a woman with three dogs and a cat, they had little more than a couple of sacks of straw on which to sleep and a rickety perambulator to carry the rest of their belongings. *Affaires* must have prospered for them, for soon there was a shaving mirror on the wall, a fur rug on the cobbled floor and a second pram garaged beside the first. Madame had also acquired a long-handled brush with which at almost every hour of the day she could be seen sweeping her hearth and door-step. The height of their elegance was reached when an inverted packing-case became a table; on it was spread not only a table-cloth but a crocheted "centre piece," and on the centre piece a vase with flowers. "Window-boxes" with geraniums also appeared on their kerb. And then one day, or one night, they moved. The only trace of their sojourn was the smoke-blackened wall where bits of scrap-iron had formed a fire-place.

But these two households were among the élite. For the most part, those of the fraternity shuffle from bridge to bridge, or from the shelter of one projecting stairway to the next, sleeping in the sun when the days are warm, wandering at night, as a badger does, to find their sustenance.

Artists on the quays are plentiful too; old and young, male and female, amateur and professional, from dawn to dusk at every season of the year. There can hardly be a bridge across the river in Paris that hasn't been painted at least once for each of its component stones. And even more oblivious of passers-by than the *clochards* or the painters are the loving couples: wandering arm in arm over the rough cobbles; standing enfolded under the arches of the bridges; sitting, seraphic, on the low coping-stones at the water's edge. Such long, long kisses, unheeding and unheeded. Isn't it wonderful the amount of emotion that can be expressed by two people without one apparent movement? It is a charming art.

One day as I was standing by a second-hand bookstall on the Quai des Grands Augustins, a rather pretty girl came up to me. In her hand was a copy of the French edition of *The Constant Nymph* by Margaret Kennedy. "Combien *La Nymphe au Coeur Fidèle*?" she asked. I could think of no better reply than "C'est sans prix, mademoiselle." What did she do but turn on her heel and go off to the other old fellow with whiskers who was the real owner of the stall.

In the seven miles of its course through Paris, the Seine has more than thirty bridges. Of these the Île de la Cité, in its length of little more than half a mile, claims ten. Five on either side, like gangways thrown from the deck of a ship whose upperworks and mast are the cathedral and its spire, they carry their endless processions of passengers and crew—pilgrims and residents of the island. The simile of a ship is an old one but inevitable.

Paris was born on the Île de la Cité. With water on either side for protection it was a natural site for a primitive settlement. There too, because of the divided stream, it was easier to span the river. From the first bridges there came into being the long straight roads which still exist—the Rue St. Martin towards Flanders in the north, the Rue St. Jacques southwards towards Spain. East and west the river was the highway. Because of its importance the badge of Paris was and still is a ship.

The district to the east of the Place St. Michel is, after the Île de la Cité, the oldest in Paris. It is a warren of narrow streets and still narrower alley-ways. The Rue du Fouarre, meaning the Street of the Straw, takes us back a thousand years to the days when the early students of learning sat there on pallets of straw while their teachers lectured from the window of an adjoining house. Education at that time being very much under the influence of the Church, the language spoken was Latin. "Better good Latin than bad Latin; better bad Latin than French" from being the rule of the schools became a fashion in the streets, hence the name Latin Quarter which survives to this day. It comprises all that district which spreads south from the river by the Île de la Cité to Montparnasse, with the Sorbonne as its centre.

I was making a drawing in the Rue St. Julien-le-Pauvre, which runs parallel to and close beside the Rue du Fouarre, when an old woman pushing a perambulator passed me and sat down on the kerb a few yards ahead. She unfastened a corner of the pram cover, and no sooner had she done so than there emerged one after the other an array of cats. I counted eight in all. One of them, an orange-and-white with one foot missing, jumped on to the kerb and sat down beside her. Another, a big marmalade tom, took up a stance on the handle of the pram. A small tabby and a black rolled on the pavement. A smoky-grey sat swishing its tail and looking expectant; a long-coated white stood by, also hopeful.

"Ah, Marcel!" said the old lady, shaking a finger at the big tom who, with tail erect and back arched, was smirking at her from his rail. "How

naughty you are! And you, *chérie*," she said to the silky grey, "you will never learn to steal, you are too beautiful for work." She took a paper bag from her pocket and began to feed them. As each animal received its scrap it took it aside to eat alone, for cats don't like conversation with meals. In this I agree with them: talk distracts from good food and good food interrupts talk. Like love-making with philosophy, the two don't mix.

As I was folding my stool to leave, I observed to the old lady that she had a big family.

"A wicked family," she answered, shaking her finger at the large tom who was again perched on the handle of the pram.

"He is very handsome," I said.

"Yes, Marcel is very handsome. I call him after my husband: he was very handsome too, with the long white moustache. He would stay out at night just like the cat, and when he came back I would be *en colère*. But then he would smile at me and I would forgive him—just like the cat."

I remarked on the orange-and-white who had lost a foot. "Ah, *le pauvre petit*, he lost the foot to a dog. He is like my daughter's son who lost a foot in the war. I call him Pierre—that is the name of my *petit-fils*. And Micheline," she said, pointing to the tortoise-shell, "lazy, lazy—she will not catch mice. Thérèse, the white, she is lazy too, but Paul-Émile—that is the black—he is good, he works very hard."

It seemed appropriate that a few moments after this encounter I should find myself in the Rue du Chat qui Pêche, a narrow alley leading to the river. How it got its name is uncertain. Some say that at one time during floods the river had free access to the cellars of the district; fish would come in with the water, and a cat of that street became famed for its skill in catching them. As I reached the quay I ran into the painter, Willy Moren. "You're wearing your Irish sweater again," he said; "some day I must paint that. When will you sit for me?" He was carrying a paint-box and was on his way to finish a portrait of a woman who lived in one of the old houses of the Île St. Louis. "She is a Rouault," he said; "outlines like a stained-glass window and colouring as fierce." I turned and walked back with him along the quay.

The pullover I was wearing was a white one that had been knitted for me in Connemara. It had a pleasant texture of cable stitch.

"White," said Willy, "is the most beautiful of all colours, the most sensitive. Yet there is no such thing as white," he added, "because white reflects everything that is around it. It is like a mirror."

I said that as an engraver my problem was to make white paper look unlike white paper, to invest it, so to speak, with colour through the medium of black ink.

"There is no such colour as black either," said Willy. "To be perceived it must be seen in light. Black seen in light is not black. Renoir called it the queen of colours."

As we were crossing the Pont de l'Archevêché, Willy stopped and leant on the parapet. "It was over here," he said with a laugh, "that Kadsine threw his first love."

"Could she swim?" I asked.

"She didn't drown," he said. "She was picked up in the mud a month later. Some men on a barge found her and sold her to a junk-shop. A bit stained but a nice carving."

"But why throw it in the river?" I asked.

"Some old professor had offered to criticize it for him—he lived where I'm going now, the Quai d'Anjou. Kadsine carried the heavy wood on his shoulders the whole way from Montparnasse; and when he unwrapped it in the big studio, all the great man did was to walk round it twice, shrug his shoulders and leave the room. Kadsine had been overworking, he was half starved too, and when he got to the bridge on his way home he was already in a fever. He threw his statue into the river and then he fainted. He was in hospital for weeks, and after that they sent him to the country. When he got back to Paris the first thing he saw as he was walking in the Rue de Seine was his own carving in the window of one of the galleries. 'I wish I knew who the artist was,' said the dealer to him. 'I can tell you,' said Kadsine, and that was the turn of his fortunes."

At the end of the bridge Willy continued his way to the Île St. Louis. I stopped awhile in the gardens that now crest the eastern prow of the larger island. Here till recently stood that sad lodging, the Morgue. Now, among the flower-beds, children play. The silence of the dead no longer reigns.

I often think that one of the saddest things about death is that the person from whom consciousness has passed knows nothing of its peace. I often think, too, that one of the happiest things about it is that the older one grows the less one fears it. How often we hear as last words, "I'm very tired." When we are sleepy we think little of the morrow.

There is great peace in old age; responsibilities have passed to others, anxiety about our choice of road in life no longer exists. We see, too, the inevitability in the sequence of many past events. What at one time seemed a climax to all adventure, was but a prelude to fresh enterprise. Unknowingly we had gone stale, had lost interest in the old activities; without realizing it, a new focus for our energy had appeared.

# CHAPTER ELEVEN

YOU wouldn't believe the smile on the face of that river when I returned to Sauvage after ten days' absence. Serene and calm as if there had never been a tantrum. The level was almost down to normal.

My boat shone blue under a clump of willows below the weir. Monsieur Cabourdin said that some friends of his had helped him to transport it. The oars and the blankets were safe in his cottage. Oh no, there was no question of reward, but he would like a picture postcard from Paris, just to say I had arrived there safely.

Now the river was as I had thought to find it at Troyes. I could move at my own pace, not at the speed dictated to me. I need no longer think of the arches of bridges as the open maws of whales and myself as mere plankton. I could go ashore and wander in sunlit fields when and where I wished. Trees athwart the river no longer mattered: I had only to slip into the water and guide the boat through the branches. And there were gravel banks for quiet contemplation. On one of them, as I boiled my first kettle on dry land, I watched a caterpillar moving with determination but with no apparent objective; again and again it fell from the pebble to which one end or the other of its anatomy had pinned faith. What else could the creature expect? It was ground unsuited to caterpillars. One trouble in life is that most of us get what we ask for, and another is that most of us are not quite sure what we are asking for. Furthermore, if anyone warns us whither we are heading, we don't like him any the better for the information.

I was awakened from a siesta by the double shot of a gun; a moment later a dog surged through the thicket on the far side of the river. But I saw no sign of game or sportsman. The best use that I ever made of gunpowder was when I was about ten years old. In a loft of the new rectory to which my father had moved I found a box of cartridges, loaded with the old black smoky powder. I opened the lot, about two dozen, and having extracted the powder I put a heap of it under the kitchen table and laid a trail from that to the back door. We had a large fat cook called Mary, in my parents' estimation a little inclined to swearing and drink but otherwise an angel. Waiting till she was bending over the table, I put a match to the end of the trail. Then I nearly died of fright. There was a rush of flame and the next moment a screeching and a swearing from the kitchen such as I'd never heard in all my ten years of life. Smoke poured out of the kitchen door into the passage where I was hiding, and through the half-open window into the stable yard. I thought it wiser to hide in a remnant of hay that had also been left behind in the loft. When next Mary saw me she came after me with a broom. "May the divil crack your bones!" I heard her shouting. She cornered me in the loose-box and was about to murder me, as I thought, when suddenly she stopped, threw her arms round me and hugged me. "Your father was wild with you," she said, "but sure, I told him 'twas only an accident."

That evening on the Seine I camped in a field with cattle grazing round me. The sky was clear, the light wind had dropped. As the sun set, reflections of pale poplar stems striped the dark water. Lying on my back and looking into the darkening heavens I saw a star's first glimmer, like a speck of dust caught in some hidden light. Its lustre grew. Then, as I looked, another glinted and caught fire, and again another. It was as though I was willing them into being. Soon there seemed no smallest space unlit... I awoke shortly before dawn. As each star faded a bird burst into song.

Now in my course appeared more and more pleasant beaches, though signs of the deluge still remained in plenty. Water-snails and mussels, cast high from their native element, gaped where they had died. In pools left by the falling water, and from which there was no escape, thousands of minnows awaited a stagnating death. On one strand where

I moored I planned a channel that would liberate a shoal of many hundreds; but before I had begun the digging two small boys appeared and with a net garnered an easy harvest. "You catch them for bait?" I asked.

"Non, monsieur," they answered, "pour s'amuser."

Snipe feeding at the water's edge took cover in the thickets. Moorhens scuttered off noisily at my approach. Kingfishers flashed ahead of me; skeins of sandpipers skimmed the surface. Eventually my so-called canal rejoined the river. "Yes, it is la *vieille Seine*," said a fisherman whom I passed with his boat moored at the junction of the two streams. Patches of purple loosestrife and yellow tufts of ragwort showed colour on the banks. Belladonna and white convolvulus climbed over flood-stained branch and twig.

A mile further on, passing under a high footbridge, I saw ahead of me the village of Marcilly bordering the far side of another river, the Aube, the greatest of the many affluents of the Seine. Rising in the same range of hills but draining a wider area of country, it is the stronger of the two rivers when they meet; yet, comparable to the Missouri at its junction with the Mississippi, it yields up its name and sinks its personality in that of the weaker partner—a phenomenon not unknown in human matrimony.

At Marcilly, thinking to have a solid meal, I went ashore and found the Hôtel Beurville. There, in the bar which is also the dining-room, Monsieur *le patron* brought me the menu. He explained that the items were *à la carte* but that I could have a meal at *prix fixe* if I preferred. As we were talking, the local postman came in and, setting down his leather sack of letters on a table, crossed over to the bar. Then, leaning across the counter, he put his arms around the girl who stood behind it, drew her towards him, and kissed her ardently on both cheeks.

"Is that *à la carte* ?" I inquired of the *patron*.

"Non, non!" he said, "en pension."

And so I arranged to stay awhile on those terms. A nice girl, Giselle, for that was her name: large dark eyes, a pretty little fringe of black curls, a retroussé nose, a merry laugh, and a silver tooth. And how she could run about in her carpet slippers among the seven tables, thirty-six chairs and a petrol pump. One Sunday evening I asked her if she wasn't tired after the long and strenuous day, with no one to help her. "Oh, mais non, ça va bien," she said. The daughter of the house puts business first.

Another evening I asked her for the loan of a knife to cut the pages of a book I was reading. What was the book about? she asked.

"Napoleon," I said, "and it's a great surprise to me," I added, "the amount of money he spent on his lady friends."

"But that was very sensible of him," she said.

"But it was money that he owed to his soldiers," I told her.

"But his soldiers did not give him so much pleasure," she answered.

"Never argue with a woman" was the only worldly advice my father ever gave me, and he was right.

Napoleon certainly did deal generously with those who gratified him in his leisure moments, and there seem to have been many of them. It is known that to one, a lady of Madrid, he gave five hundred napoleons, the equivalent of more than £2,000 today, for but an evening's entertainment. To a valet who on another occasion had acted successfully as an intermediary he gave more than half that sum. Contrariwise, he could be extremely parsimonious when it came to the expenditure of a few francs by one of his workmen. But of all his favours, perhaps it was those to his generals which cost him most. In 1813 Marshal Oudinot appeared to advocate making peace with

England and the Allies. Only after long discussions with his Emperor did he say: "Sire, you are not as generous as you used to be: you are becoming miserly." Napoleon took the hint. "Nous verrons," he replied. A few days later he sent to Oudinot the equivalent of £75,000 in present currency. When next the subject of an attack was mentioned Oudinot was eager for battle. "Your Majesty understands me," he said. A short while before Waterloo, the Marshal Soult also became pacifist until he had received "a vast encouragement."

It is an interesting sidelight on Napoleon's character that when, as he sometimes would, he played dice with his soldiers, he always pocketed his winnings. It is another that once when a beautiful young girl came to his château, having misunderstood the purpose of his invitation, he sent her away as innocent as when he had welcomed her and with the promise of a considerable dowry.

A strange idiosyncrasy of the emperor's was that though he was accustomed to souse himself with eau-de-Cologne, he could not abide strong perfumes, a trait that sometimes led to complications in his amours. Constant, his valet, tells us in his memoirs how on one occasion he was summoned to the presence by a ringing of the bell as if to break its cord. He found the lady in one room and Napoleon in another. "Constant," cried the Emperor, "take this girl away! She will kill me with her perfumes, they are unbearable. Open all the windows and the doors. Above all, take her away quickly!" The lady, needless to say, was not a little upset, though a handsome present dried her tears. When Constant returned from his escort duty he found Napoleon still sitting pale and dishevelled where he had left him, mopping his brow with eau-de-Cologne.

Oddly enough, the painter Degas had the same aversion to scents. He even hated flowers on account of their perfume, and when walking in public gardens would choose paths that were bordered only by lawns. When lunching or dining with friends, he would take the flowers from the table and put them in some far corner of the room. He would become irritable and even offensive if a woman brought flowers into a bus in which he was travelling.

# CHAPTER TWELVE

DECISIONS are often made for us. I was sitting on my sketching-stool by the edge of the canal that enters the Aube just above its junction with the Seine, and I was wondering if I would take the stool with me on a small jaunt that I had thought of for later in the day. All of a sudden I found myself on the flat of my back. A leg of the stool had bust. That saved further argument. Life is full of surprises. Only this year they chose my birthday as Mothering Sunday, yet no one mothered me. I could have done with a mother that day by the canal to mend a split in my trousers after the accident.

The same afternoon on the bridge across the Aube at Saron, a couple of miles upstream, I was lamenting my loss when an elderly farmer in dusty, heavily patched clothes, carrying a large sack on his back, stopped beside me. He dropped his burden to the ground and began to talk. Yes, indeed, he said, the *inondations* had been severe. He had lost millions of beetroots. And they had been doing well; they were as big as your thumb before the floods came. But he was lucky, he explained, because he had two farms, one in the valley, the other on high ground. The beetroots on the high ground would be very good; men from Brittany would come to pull them—they would earn a thousand francs a day in addition to their food and lodging.

I asked him if there was a buvette in the village, for the sun was fierce.

"*Une* buvette?" he queried with surprise. There were three in the village. But why did I ask? Was I thirsty? Then I must come to his house; it wasn't a hundred metres from the bridge. He picked up his sack and led me towards the village.

We had gone scarcely fifty yards when he opened a pair of iron gates on our left and threw his sack inside. That was his son's farm, he said. Then we crossed the road, went through a wicket gate and into a garden, and here I was introduced to his wife, as spherical in form as he was angular. He took me indoors and after a few minutes' chat went into the next room to change his clothes, giving orders to his wife that she was to open a bottle of wine.

The good lady wasn't quite sure whether her lord had said red or white wine. She seemed to feel also that I must not be left alone. And so while I sat on a chair by the door and she stood by the fire-place nervously fingering the highly polished copper pots and pans that stood along the mantelshelf, we discussed, inevitably, the rising price of food, with Monsieur joining in our conversation through the thin partition. In due course he reappeared, transformed in smart navy blue. Madame, with more explicit instructions, went to the cellar and brought back a bottle of white wine, Aligoté '47, a cool and comfortable drink. Monsieur inquired about conditions in England and compared them with those in France. "We in France suffered most during the war," he said: "now it is in England that they are suffering." But how fortunate the English were to have a royal family—a republic was a great mistake. The president of a republic was only there for a few years and he had to gather for himself all he could in that short time, but a king and queen were there always, for life, and they had to make the best they could of the country for their children who would come after.

When at last I insisted that I must move he came with me through the village. He wanted to show me his herd of black-and-white Dutch cattle, the breed that he most favoured. They were in the stalls when we reached his farm, and it pleased him greatly when I remarked on the milking by machinery. He was very proud of this installation. He said that when he was a young man he could buy a cow for four thousand francs; now a good one cost a hundred and fifty thousand. From the farm he came with me as far as the cross-roads, where he put me on the straight road to Anglure, three miles higher up the Aube.

"If ever you come back," he said, "you will find the doors of my house *grandes ouvertes.*"

A Baron d'Anglure was among those who, during the first Crusade, were taken prisoner by the troops of Saladin and held to ransom. "If I may but visit my château on the Aube," he said to the sultan, "I will

return with the money." Saladin granted his request. Alas, when he reached home he found little in the coffers: Madame la Baronne had been entertaining too lavishly during his absence. As sad as he was empty-handed, he returned to the sultan. "I have no money," he said, "I have only my word. *Me voici!*" Saladin, pleased with such integrity, then gave him his freedom on three conditions: that the Seigneurs d'Anglure would always bear the name of Saladin, that the arms of Anglure would always carry the crescent of Islam and that the baron would build two mosques in his native country. And so it came about. The name of Saladin is borne as a Christian name by all male members of the family; the shield of the family is "D'or semé de grelots d'argt soutenus chacun par un croissant de gue," of gold sown with silver bells, each one supported by a red crescent; and of the mosques, one stands, a tower with an Eastern cupola as roof, attached to the church at the neighbouring village of Clesles. It is known as La Tour des Fromages since at one time the cupola was used as a drying loft for the newly made Camembert and other soft cheeses of the district. The other mosque is at Bourlemont in the Ardennes.

Saladin has been described as "a saint who realized in his personality the highest virtues and ideals of Mohammedanism." Stanley Lane-Poole in his Life of the sultan wrote: "If the taking of Jerusalem were the only feat known about Saladin, it were enough to prove him the most chivalrous and great-hearted conqueror of his own, and perhaps of any, age."

As an instance of the courtesy shown to each other by combatants at that time it is related that at the siege of Kerak, a town some twenty miles from the south-eastern shore of the Dead Sea, the troops of Saladin, after months of attack and repulse, had forced their way into the town and there remained only the citadel to be taken. But it happened that just then a wedding was being celebrated in the castle and the noise of battle would have been an inconvenience for both bride and groom and out of place for all. So the French commander, one Reginald de Châtillon, sent a gift of meat and wine to Saladin, as it were a share of the bride-cake. Saladin for reply gave orders to all commanders of his artillery that the bridal tower was in no way to be molested. It is sad to relate that later, Saladin, infuriated by the continued treacheries of the same Reginald, swore to kill him with his own hand and, when opportunity arose, carried out his threat.

A woman in Ireland once said to me: "Isn't it hard to keep your thoughts on the altar when the fellow you're fond of is in the seat behind you." Her words came into my mind when, after a few days at Marcilly, my thoughts began to wander from the river and to make their way to a town some fifty miles behind me to the north, the town of Reims. Visions of tight-waisted corks began to appear before my eyes, and in my day-dreams I would hear clear bell-like notes and bubbling music. I wonder if any performer on harp, sackbut, psaltery or any other kind of instrument has ever struck as gladsome a sound as that made by a cork when leaving a champagne bottle. What other single note in this world has such power to hush a crowd to silence or wake a silent man to speech? And there isn't even a mention of it in the *Oxford Companion to Music*.

Now that's a wonderful book. If it wasn't for its size and weight it would be one of the happiest of bedside volumes. Listen to what it says about Paderewski, after reference to his dazzling technique: "By this possession, and by those of a romantic personality, high interpretative qualities and an amazing head of hair, he established a position with the crowd and with the connoisseurs." And of Dame Ethel Smyth: "It is the opinion of some that had she been a man she would have been enabled more quickly to make her mark as a conductor, and of others that she could with difficulty have made it at all." Are there not nice morsels of insight behind those two statements? From Abdominal breathing and Acoustics under "A," by way of Bach and Bagpipes under "B" and Cancans and Cantatas under "C," the volume leads us through the whole alphabetical gamut of musical information until, after more than a thousand pages, it informs us as a finish that *zweiunddreissigstel* is German for a thirty-second, and that a Zymbalum is a Hungarian dulcimer.

Days went by at Marcilly. The unrest upon me grew. I mustn't let it become a neurosis, I thought. I had one introduction to the house of

Krug and another to Pommery and Greno. And I remembered, too, that no less an authority than my friend André Simon had described champagne as "the safest medicine in all cases of exhaustion, a lifesaving agent that will bring relief when all else has failed." Hadn't I lost pounds in weight in my battling with the flood? It might be the beginning of a decline. And, after all, I hadn't come to France to *drink* the Seine. I discovered that there was a bus direct from Anglure to Reims.

My first call was to Pommery Park: above ground, a Victorian mansion; below it, antres vast as any that Othello knew, cavern after cavern, dimly lit, with shadowed arcades leading from one to another.

"The big caves were dug by the Romans when they needed stone for building the city," said my guide. "There are eleven miles of galleries between them."

"And how many bottles?" I asked.

"Only eight million now," he said apologetically. "There used to be twelve million before the war."

At a hundred feet below the surface there is no vibration from traffic overhead, there is no change in temperature, there is no change in anything but the wine which day and night grows more and more mature—a wonderful advertisement for idleness. I rested that afternoon.

On the next morning Monsieur Joseph Krug himself, old enough to be my father, young enough to be my son, conducted me through the cellars of Maison Krug. The care with which he selected a candlestick for me and the gentle courtesy with which he placed it in my hand took my thoughts back to when my grandfather, in his study full of curios, would choose from his collection of arrowheads one that he thought would make a brooch for some particular lady. He had a big collection of these arrowheads, in flint, in quartz, in obsidian, and he made many such presentations. I used to wonder why he chose arrowheads.

It was midsummer when I visited Reims and there was, of course, no sign either of ripe grapes in the vineyards or of new wine coming from the presses. But that didn't detract in any way from the pleasure of walking in cool cloisters, so richly furnished, or from the aesthetic discussions that took place afterwards.

In one sector of the labyrinth, Monsieur Krug showed me many racks of bottles at which men were at work. The bottles were tilted head downwards, the angle varying from rack to rack, and the men were giving each bottle a slight sideways turn to the right. "In the making of champagne," said Monsieur Krug, "there are two fermentations, the first after the natural grape-juice, the *must*, has been put into casks to become wine, the second after that wine has been put into bottles to mature. During each fermentation sediment is formed. It does not matter in the casks because it is left behind when the wine is drawn off—we call it the *lees*—but it does matter in the bottles because one of the charms of champagne is its clarity. This is how we remove it."

He then explained that, after being drawn from the cask, the wine in its bottles is left untouched for several years, the bottles lying on their sides. During that time the second fermentation takes place and the resultant sediment settles on the underside of the bottles. He took one that had been almost horizontal in its rack and showed me a faint streak of cloudiness along its lower side. "We don't want that on the dinner table," he said. "The problem is to get it out." Then he said that after four, five, or six years of resting, the bottles are moved to these racks and at regular intervals are tilted to steeper and steeper angles, until eventually they are standing vertical, inverted. And during that time they have also been gently rotated. "That is what the men are doing now," he said. He pointed to a dab of white paint on the bottom of each bottle. "That is the guide. Today it has reached seven o'clock. In a few days it will have reached nine. When it gets back to twelve o'clock it will have made a complete circle, then it will be ready." As we moved from one of the galleries into a vast hall he said to me: "Now here we will see the *dégorgement*, the expulsion of the sediment." He picked out a bottle from where it had been standing on its head, and held it up to the light. The contents were crystal clear but resting on the end of the cork was about half an inch of sediment.

In the centre of the cave was a large shallow trough filled with bottles that stood head down with their necks through a grating. "Freezing mixture," said Monsieur Krug. "Only the cork and the sediment are in contact." A man sitting beside a machine leant forward and took a bottle from the trough. He turned it right way up, released the cork. *Pop*—and with the cork there had been blown a frozen pellet of sediment. The machine was ready with another cork, a woman was ready with a metal cap and some wire, and quicker than I could follow the movements, the bottle was ready for its tinsel paper and its label.

"I wonder whose wedding that will be cheering," I said to Monsieur Krug.

"Maybe a publisher will be celebrating a success," he said, smiling.

# CHAPTER THIRTEEN

I SAID good-bye to Monsieur Beurville and his wife, to Giselle and the postman, and once again I launched forth on to the river. The wide seat of my boat was luxury after the narrow slatted chairs at the hotel. Many a time had my flesh yearned and my bones creaked for even a fragment of a cushion, let alone an arm-chair. It was a constant surprise to me that in so many of the smaller hotels in France they see no need for such a comfort. "Oh yes," said Madame, "you will find them in the big hotels on the Côte d'Azur, and there are beach chairs on the plages by the river, but not in the small hotels. We have *les parasols* but not *les fauteuils.*" It seemed that for once in France there was something that was "not done." As is often the case, the "not doing" causes a lot of discomfort.

Now the river ran softly as the Thames. It was no longer *la Petite Seine*, it was no longer even *une rivière*, with moments of "shaller-water prattle": since its junction with the Aube it had become, writ clear on all the charts, *Seine Fleuve.* There was time to watch the bottle-green dragonflies flickering among reeds whose tips were emerald in the sunlight, whose shadowed stems were smoky blue; time to contemplate the flotsam that had accumulated on a flood-torn branch and from which already new life was springing—maybe the birth of an island; time to listen to the notes of doves, or follow the scrounging of a rat at the water's edge. Powder-blue butterflies, small bronze butterflies, whites whose wings were tipped with orange, whites whose wings were veined with black, and golden fritillaries; swathes of buttercup-yellow water lilies; a girl in scarlet, sunlit on a bridge; a lemon boat with a fisherman in blue.

There were fishermen everywhere, legions of them, sitting or standing, comatose, content. At times it seemed as if reeds grew only to camouflage rods. And there was scarcely a stretch of river that hadn't got its *bateau pêche* tied to stakes. How the river could sustain its stocks seemed to me a major mystery, for these fishermen do catch fish. Day and night thousands of them, from bank or boat, keep everything that hooks itself, great or small. One early morning, when the only light was from the moon in its last quarter, I heard human voices. Dew was thick on the gunwale of the boat, my blanket was furred with moisture, and a grey mist shrouded the river. I thought perhaps some farmer with his cowherd must be abroad early to attend to a sick animal. Then, peering into the mist, I distinguished two dim figures on the water. They were sitting on chairs on a raft, moored to posts in midstream, and each had two rods.

"Have no fear, monsieur," said a man late one night, having tripped over my mooring rope and dived into a bed of rushes close to the boat. No, he wasn't hurt; it was only the possible damage to his rod that worried him. But he had dropped it as he fell, and it lay on the ground unharmed. Next morning I found two dead perch among the broken rushes. They must have slithered from his basket.

Another day I passed a magnificent launch with a houseboat trailing after it. The owner leant over his polished rail and offered me a large pike which he had just caught and didn't want. Like the small boys higher upstream he was merely killing fish "pour s'amuser."

The calm of my journey was now broken only by the weirs which regulated the waters of the canals. Each one meant a portage, and the boat was heavy. But just as in the upper areas a figure had always loomed up, as if from nowhere, to help me in my difficulties, so in these middle reaches sooner or later someone would appear, ready and anxious to render "un service." It might mean finding a couple of poles as rollers for overland transport, or it might even mean going half a mile to the nearest village to find a "camarade" to help—in which case, was there nothing from the shops that could be fetched for me at the same time?

Some twelve miles below Marcilly I reached Nogent, and there I went ashore to seek the tomb of Héloïse and Abelard. Their sad history, taking us back to the twelfth century, is well known. Helen Waddell has made of it a tender and moving romance; George Moore has done likewise. Roger Lloyd has sought in more factual prose "to reanimate the still dust of two immortals." He describes Abelard as physically beautiful, gay, and pleasant in manner, quick of intellect, well read, capacious of memory, a master of logical argument and of metaphysics, a poet. He says that to be in his company was felt to be an honour, and he quotes an enemy of Abelard who could not but admit: "He is sublime in Eloquence."

Héloïse, niece of Fulbert, an aged canon of Notre-Dame, was a pupil of Abelard. Tall and fair, of striking presence, and "in the abundance of her learning, supreme," she fell in love with him. No blame to her if her guardian, ambitious for his niece's reputation as a scholar, took Abelard into his house to be her tutor. Little blame to her if, subject to her tutor's "eloquence," she became subject also to his love. In one of her letters to him—letters that have been superbly translated by Charles Scott Moncrieff—she wrote: "There are two things, I confess, in thee especially wherewith thou couldst at once captivate the heart of any woman, namely the arts of making songs and of singing them."

There came a time when Héloïse, "with the greatest exultation," found that she was with child. We have no evidence that Abelard also exulted, indeed there seems much to show that his feelings were to the contrary. This would complicate his life still more. We find no trace of that added tenderness which most men feel when the woman they love has conceived. It would seem that not for any great love did he marry her after the birth of his son, but to appease Fulbert, her uncle.

It was typical of Héloïse that she should have been against the marriage. Her thoughts were only for Abelard and the brilliant future which she foresaw for him. She knew that marriage would shatter the possibility of his promotion to high office in the church, and she did her utmost to dissuade him from it. As she wrote to him some years later: "Nothing have I ever (God wot) required of thee save thyself, desiring thee purely, not what was thine. Not for the pledge of matrimony, nor for any dowry did I look, nor my own passions or wishes but thine (as thou thyself knowest) was I zealous to gratify... I call God to witness, if Augustus ruling over the whole world, were to deem me worthy of the honour of marriage, and to confirm the whole world to me, to be ruled by me for ever, dearer to me and of greater dignity would it seem to be called thy strumpet than his empress."

In order that the marriage might at any rate be kept secret, they parted after the ceremony, Héloïse returning to her uncle's house and Abelard to his former lodging. But such secrets are not easily kept. Rumours turned to gossip, and gossip began to spread. It was bound to injure Abelard. After long deliberation they reached the decision that Héloïse should enter a convent: this, they felt, would be tantamount to annulment of the marriage and should therefore allay the growing hostility. Abelard took her to the convent at Argenteuil where she had spent many of her childhood years, and there he handed her over to the abbess. One might have expected that this would have satisfied Fulbert. Far from it: behind a mask of forgiveness he nursed an ever-growing hatred of Abelard and a desire to injure him. In his eyes, the fact that Héloïse had entered a convent might well have removed those obstacles to Abelard's ordination as priest that had arisen from his marriage, and it was this ordination, carrying with it in Abelard's case almost a certainty of subsequent high preferment, that Fulbert wished of all things to frustrate. He remembered the qualifications for priesthood laid down in the Book of Deuteronomy, and in the darkness of his soul he devised a means by which Abelard would be for ever debarred from the order of priesthood. Late at night, under Fulbert's orders, men entered Abelard's room and inflicted upon him the most degrading mutilation that man can suffer.

Now our sympathies go out to Abelard. It is well known that such misfortune affects not only a man's body but his mind, perverting his thoughts as it torments his flesh. We must not be hasty to judge a man thus afflicted from the letters he wrote to Héloïse after years of suffering. Even when he penned such sentences as: "For such renown had I then, and so excelled in grace of youth and form, that I feared no refusal from whatever woman I might deem worthy of my love," we must consider whether the words came not from vanity but from a mind borne down with humiliation, seeking to recover some fragment of its self-esteem. If in his letters there appears a cruelty to the memory of his love, a cruelty that must have torn the heart strings of the woman whose selfless devotion to him endured to the last, we must be compassionate.

Héloïse's letters to Abelard express a love as intemperate in passion as it was exalted in abnegation. "So sweet to me," she wrote, "were those delights of lovers which we enjoyed in common that they cannot either displease me nor hardly pass from my memory... When I ought to lament for what I have done I sigh rather for what I have had to forgo." And at another time: "In the whole period of my life," she writes, "I have ever feared to offend thee rather than God, I seek to please thee more than Him. Thy command brought me, not the love of God, to the habit of religion."

Abelard died in 1142, some thirteen years after he had installed Héloïse as abbess in the convent near Nogent which he had dedicated to "Le Paraclet," the Holy Spirit, the Comforter, a refuge where during a few years of his restless life he had lived and taught. His body was brought there and buried in the crypt of the oratory. When twenty-two years later Héloïse died, she also was laid in the same crypt. There are some who say that their bodies were not allowed to lie beside each other. I do not know. When I visited the site of the convent—the buildings are no more—I was shown a vault wherein under its ivy-covered roof the bodies were said to have rested. It matters little to either of them now whether or not they shared that same damp cell. I fear it matters as little that today their mingled ashes lie in one tomb, in the cemetery of Père Lachaise in Paris.

# CHAPTER FOURTEEN

IN THE regions below Nogent there were many signs of the recent *inondations* which, according to local accounts, had been not only *véritablement inquiétantes* but in places *catastrophiques*. If the reeds on either bank were not weighed down with a coating of white silt, they were brown and seared as if by a flame. Fishing-boats had been lifted and thrown awry against the banks; others, submerged, still hung on their mooring ropes. Eel traps, long tubular contrivances of lattice wire, had been torn from the river-bed and lay wantonly among the reeds, high above river level. In one of these I noticed two water-rails who through some freak of fancy had found their way into its innermost chamber. But for my interference they must have died a lingering death. What exquisite little creatures these rails are! So slender of build; shy, elusive, more often heard than seen, the olive green of their backs and grey of their throat and breast merging with the grey-green of their marshy haunts. I had often heard their call at night, a sharp *kik-kik-kik*, but till then had never held one in my hand. Yet I had no heart to prolong even momentarily their captivity. They fluttered as I cut the wire, they were quiet when I took them in my hand, they scampered into cover with polite but undisguised delight when I set them free.

Not far from the village of Courceroy a small boy in a home-made canoe, flying a black flag with a skull and crossbones, shot out of a backwater a short distance ahead of me. He crossed my bows, circled my boat, raised his paddle in salute and disappeared again into his creek. I wondered what dreams of piracy and privateering were in his head, and was reminded of another boy who had been more given to boat-building than scholastic effort. It happened that one day I had to discuss with him some of the finer points of education, for he had been to one of the more modern schools in England and I was a bit doubtful of his progress. He was eleven years old at the time. I began with arithmetic.

"You know your tables, of course, up to twelve times," I suggested.

"Not exactly all," he said.

"Up to ten times, then?"

"Not quite up to ten times."

"Well, how far do you know?"

"I used to know up to three times," he said thoughtfully.

Hoping to find a happier subject, I asked: "Can you tell me the difference between a noun and a verb?"

"I'm no good at maths," he said.

Yet a few years later that boy was navigating lieutenant in a ship of war.

"How did you manage about the maths?" I asked.

"They're exciting when you're interested," he said.

And a mile or so further down, where at a bend of the river the road almost touches the water's edge, a young man with a limp made me think of a story I had heard in Paris. The parents of a young soldier had been living apart for several years, and the boy had been reported missing. No other news of him had come to them since that first intimation. Yet after the armistice had been signed and train-loads of returning prisoners were arriving daily, both mother and father would go morning after morning, evening after evening, to the terminus in hopes that they might find their son. They did not speak to each other, they stood there silent and apart, watching the happiness of other reunions. Weeks passed, months passed. It seemed that there were no more to come back from across the frontier. Still the two were there, standing apart. Then one evening, without speaking, he took her arm

and he went back with her to their old home. He found everything just as when he had gone away, even his chair beside the table. He stayed there that night, and once again each felt the comfort of the other's body. And in the morning as they slept late, for they had no longer any hope, the door opened and their son came in.

Poplars everywhere. Like the willows, they are so irregular in their mating habits that to keep the strain pure they have to be propagated by cuttings. Even trees, it seems, are promiscuous. But subject to this chastening of their nature, their timber being tough is suitable for the frameworks of houses and, being light also, for packing-cases, fruit baskets, cheese-boxes and three-ply. Along the banks of the Seine these trees are cultivated as carefully as bean rows in an English garden. It was because of the innumerable straight lines of them, at every angle, in the upper flood that I never knew whether I was on or off the river.

These were tranquil days in the boat. There were mornings when, casting off at dawn, I drifted through long cool shadows, watching the sunlight on the trees creep down to meet the water, hearing no sound but the tremolo of the aspens, seeing no one but a chance sportsman and his dog. There were noons with cooling breezes and flocculent clouds high in the sky, and evenings when the forest rang with bird song and the river was a sheet of moving glass. There were nights when, looking skywards, the passing clouds seemed like new continents and islands marked on the inside of a mighty globe.

Hereabouts there was just enough current to keep me moving through the stretches of restful, unexciting landscape. I could relax and let fancies flitter through my brain as inconsequentially as a ladybird or a drowsy moth might rest a moment on the gunwale.

The trouble with just "being" is that you get nothing done. The trouble with "doing" is that it makes you unconscious of "being." Nothing is worth doing unless you concentrate your thoughts upon it, yet if you do that you miss the consciousness of the doing, and enjoy only the having done.

At Grisy it seemed that my chart had gone wrong. Perhaps I was "being" too much and not attending to the "doing." I met a lock where no such hindrance should have been, and a mountain of a female lock-keeper who said I must go back to Troyes for a permit to pass through. But my pocket was nearer than Troyes, and in it I discovered a permit, of standard pattern, which opened all gates.

Below the lock I saw an old woman kneeling at her washing-board, and I found myself making a drawing of her. And as I was finishing it a barge appeared round the bend ahead, hooting as it came to warn the lock-keeper of its approach—the first barge I had met on the river. And, with the pencil still in my hand, I made a quick note of its lines, and then of those of a girl aboard it who was hanging out clothes, and when they had both vanished into the lock I noticed a pleasant clump of reeds beside me and I drew that. So before that day was over there I was with a bit of "doing" done after all.

# CHAPTER FIFTEEN

AFTER three days' journeying from Nogent I reached the town of Montereau, where in February 1814, six weeks before his abdication, Napoleon won almost his last victory over the Allies. Here the Seine is joined by the Yonne, perhaps the loveliest of all its tributaries. Bridges across the two rivers meet on the last foothold of dividing land, and there in bronze glory rides the Emperor.

What with the arches of the two bridges and the monument at their junction, I thought of the Arc de Triomphe in Paris and of how, if an alternative idea of Napoleon's had matured, that great arch would never have existed but, instead, a gigantic elephant, some two hundred and fifty feet in height, would have dominated the Champs Elysées. Napoleon considered that this would be a symbol of his campaign in Egypt and an appropriate memorial to the victories of *la Grande Armée*. Four great rooms within, connected by an ornate staircase, would hold trophies of his battles. Surmounting all would be a royal statue. To please those who felt that a fountain might be a more decorative feature in the landscape, he planned that water should spout from the pachyderm's trunk. Fortunately for Paris, and the world, the Emperor changed his mind and decided on the arch, though that did not prevent him having a plaster model of the elephant set up in the Place de la Bastille. There for a time it stood and crumbled, being used as a shelter by the homeless.

Sad to say, Napoleon never saw the finished Arc. Though the first stone of it was laid on his birthday in 1806 it did not reach completion until thirty years later. Changes in the country's constitution, not to mention arguments among the architects, delayed its construction. In 1810, when the Emperor married Marie-Louise and, on her entry into the city, would fain have displayed this effort of his imagination, the foundations were still scarcely above ground level. Nothing daunted, however, he gave orders that a facsimile of what was yet to be should be constructed of timber and canvas: scene-painters would produce the necessary bas-reliefs. Three weeks only it took to set the stage. It had all the appearance of reality. But the nearby site chosen for the display of fireworks had to be abandoned for one at a greater distance lest at a crucial moment the "monument" should go up in flames.

Below Montereau the character of the river changes. The landscape is dominated by pylons and factory chimneys; there is a railway on either side and there are numerous piers to which barges are moored. Augmented by the waters of the Yonne, the river has become so wide that it resembles a long and winding lake; to gain any advantage from the current I had to steer a course remote from either shore. Inside the two enormous locks that followed within a few miles of each other, I felt like an earwig in a bath.

Below Vernon the water was marbled with oil stains and the air was pungent with vapours from a petroleum depot. From there to St. Mammes, another mile, the banks were lined with barges.

St. Mammes is a port of assembly and dispersal for these barges. Some travel the upper Seine as far as Marcilly, others navigate the Canal du Loing and reach Orleans and the Loire. Others again make their way up the Yonne from Montereau and, using its tributary canals, attain the heart of Burgundy and beyond. On either side of the river these massive bluff-bowed craft lined the banks, lying alongside each other five or six deep in places. Many of their decks were gay with flowers in pots and boxes, some carried horses in their holds, nearly all had dogs. I saw women swabbing down the decks, men tarring the sides, girls handling coils of steel cables as if they were skeins of thread, small children swarming around their large mammas, lines of washing flapping in the wind.

The Loing flows into the Seine at St. Mammes. I rowed a few yards up the stream and went ashore in search of provender. Just across the quay from where I had moored, I found a cool and fragrant garden with tables set for déjeuner. Why open a tin of sardines in the sun, I asked myself, when fresh trout are being offered in the shade?

The *patron* was much interested in my voyage and my drawings. He showed me his collection of paintings by local artists of which he was rightly proud, and then he spoke of Alfred Sisley. "You know his painting of St. Mammes?" he asked. "It is in the Louvre now. Certainly it is the finest of all his work—the colour more brilliant, more luminous even than his *Inondations à Marly*. Beside him, Monet himself seems subdued in colour. That line of shadowed houses in his St. Mammes picture—they float like a mirage between sky and river."

His wife, seated in the shade beside the door of her kitchen, looked up from the *haricots verts* she was preparing.

"Of course, when Sisley made that picture the trees had not been planted, you understand—now we have a fine row of trees all the length of our waterfront," she said.

"For twenty years he lived in Moret," said the *patron*. "You are going there, of course? It is no more than a mile from here—on the River Loing, not the Seine." He urged me not to miss it, saying it was nothing of a walk. He would look after the boat for me while I was away, and if I wanted to stay there overnight he would bring my belongings ashore and keep them for me until I returned.

And so an hour later, with a haversack on my back, I reached Moret-sur-Loing. It would be difficult to find any other two towns so near to each other in distance and yet so far removed in time as the one I had but just left and the one in which I now found myself. Moret with its medieval towers and arches, narrow streets and paved alley-ways, astride a comely stream margined with lawns and ornamental trees; St. Mammes, a single long waterfront, whose shops cater only for the needs of barges and their inhabitants—"Fournitures pour la Marine," "Épicerie du Port," "Bazar du Quai." Moret with the scent of roses in the air, St. Mammes perfumed only by the oil depot.

"*Pauvre* Sisley! He was so unhappy—always, always so poor. He wore sabots because he could not afford shoes. He could not even buy potatoes for his children because no one would give him credit, no one would take his pictures in exchange for food. Then when he died, the very day after, his pictures sell for big prices." So I was told by an old lady who remembered the artist in his last years.

"*Pauvre* Sisley," she continued. "He asked that when he died, only a rough stone of the forest he loved so well should mark his tomb. So this was done, and a few days later when they took some flowers to lay there, they found around the stone the marks of rabbits' feet. His little friends from the forest had been to visit him."

Sisley, born in Paris in 1839 of English parents, had even more difficulty in selling his pictures than most of his fellow Impressionists. In 1878 he wrote to his friend Théodore Duret, the journalist and critic, begging him to find someone who in exchange for thirty pictures would give him even five hundred francs a month for six months, a total of three thousand francs. No one responded. Yet within a year of the artist's death in 1899 less than thirty pictures from his studio fetched a total of one hundred and twelve thousand francs, and in the year following a single canvas of his was bought for forty-three thousand francs.

For the last twenty years of his life Sisley lived at Moret, painting the river there, its mills and bridges. He has been called "the poet of placid streams." "No one has better shown how objects are enveloped in luminous vibration, or how the quality of light alters the form of things." He painted the river constantly but as a mirror for the sky. He painted the weather, the seasons, light and air, mist and snow and rain. Often one has the feeling that he worked at tremendous speed, as if the colours on his palette leapt into place at the first touch of his brush.

Sitting by the river at Moret I watched fishermen in gaily painted punts, scarlet and crocus-yellow and ultramarine, anchored in midstream. Naked boys were bathing at the weir, their brown skins glowing in the sunlight like ripe chestnuts. Weeping willows dripped their apple-green reflections into the mottled sky-reflecting water. It was a shimmering mosaic of pointilliste colour.

Pointillism, the method of painting in which the pigment is applied in small touches of prismatic colour, is a particularly happy technique for the rendering of sparkling light. In contrast to the broad and gallant strokes that need so much assurance and often suffer from retouching, it enables the artist slowly and meditatively to clarify and emphasize his intention. Dreaming through half-closed eyes, he can sense the result of

even one added speck of pigment; it may be dark to give greater glory to the light, it may be light to illuminate the dark; it may be an accent of orange or vermilion to startle and bring forward, it may be a note of blue or green to beget calm and contrive recession.

In the early summer of 1914, when my ambition was still to be a painter, I did a small picture in this manner, and because I liked it a little I gave it to a girl I liked very much. A year later when, after a trip to the Dardanelles and unknown to her, I was passing her flat in London on my way to hospital, the cord of my picture broke and it fell to the ground. "Bob is wounded," she said to a mutual friend who was with her in the room.

It would seem that everyone in Moret is a fisherman, that every shop has an interest in fishing. There are rods for sale in the Pharmacie, baits displayed in the Librairie; the grocer, the haberdasher and the hairdresser all deal in "Articles de Pêche." And everyone is prepared to discuss the finer points of the art, and to elaborate on his own methods of reaching success, from the small boy catching chub from the bridge with a bait of red cherries to the connoisseur who casts a fly for trout on to the dark pools beside the weir. Bream, roach, perch, tench, carp, barbel, pike and trout—all are sought for and all are caught in amazing numbers. "The Loing is the most 'poissoneuse rivière' in all France," one of the fishermen assured me.

Chub are voracious feeders, enjoying anything from worms, crickets and grasshoppers to minnows, frogs and water rats with, on occasion, a moulting crayfish; as a seasonal variation they are not averse to the seeds and roots of water-plants. Why they feel passionate about crimson cherries, which must surely be foreign to their habitat, I do not know, though doubtless they themselves have good reason. At one time we wondered why the salmon in our rivers preferred boiled shrimps to those of "a natural colour"; now we know that in the depths of the ocean, whither salmon resort to build up their strength after spawning, the shrimps on which they feed are red and not the pale greenish shade of coastal waters. One day perhaps we shall know how cats developed a liking for fish, the product of an element so abhorrent to their natures. We may learn, too, how certain species of spiders developed a similar taste—many instances have been recorded in America of them dropping from overhanging branches on to their unsuspecting quarry in the water and, after biting them behind the head, manoeuvring them to the shore and eating them.

For the casual amateur of chub fishing, the baits which I have mentioned will be found sufficiently varied, but for anyone wishing to devote himself to the calling it is as well that he should carry his study further. I therefore add a few recipes which I culled during my short stay in Moret. Quite the first choice of bait should be the scrapings of a pig's intestine; failing that, bits of a calf's stomach or of its brain, or pellets of clotted blood, will be found almost equally tempting. Alternatively the chopped-up intestines of birds, especially game birds, bring excellent results. But in respect of the latter, as the guts of game birds are not always at hand when one wishes for a quiet hour of fishing, it is well to instruct your cook, scullery maid or wife that when a bird has been killed for the table she is to put its "innards" on one side "that they may be made into a conserve"—I quote from the text-book. Then as soon as the precious entrails are in your possession you pass them between two splints of wood, held lightly between the fingers, in order to cleanse them thoroughly. Now it only remains to cut them into short lengths, scald for half an hour, and then soak in cold water for five or six hours. After that leave them overnight on a cloth to dry. In the morning, put them into a stoneware jar with a little coarse salt, a little moist sugar and

a few leaves of thyme and laurel. Put a weight on top and cover the jar. And when you have done all that and rested awhile, you go out and catch a fish that because of the insipid taste of its flesh and its bony framework isn't worth eating.

The variety of fish in the Loing is only equalled by the variety of mushrooms found in the neighbouring country that *are* worth eating. Many of them are known though little appreciated in England: the trumpet-shaped *Corne d'Abondance*, sometimes called *La Trompette de la Mort* because of its funereal colouring, becomes the Horn of Plenty in England; the more inviting yellow trumpets, *Les Chanterelles*, retain their pretty name on this side of the Channel; not so *Les Pieds Rouges* which are here designated Ruddy Warty Caps. Our Parasol and Milk mushrooms, our Blewits and our Morels, are all found at Moret in profusion but, unlike the practice in this country of leaving them to rot where they grow, in France they are gathered with care and grace the feasts of epicures.

There is no shortage of historical interest in Moret. Kings and princes in plenty have lived or halted there. St. Thomas à Becket consecrated its church; Napoleon spent the night of 19th March 1815 in the town after his escape from Elba. It is still remembered how, in an absent-minded moment, he made use of a porcelain vase, a precious heirloom of his host's, for a purpose other than the decoration for which it had been intended. His hostess's exclamation when, after his departure, she realized what had happened, is also remembered. The epithet is spelt the same in both French and English—with a line of dots.

Jacqueline de Bueil, who for reasons best known to herself and Henri IV, was created by him Comtesse de Moret and given a mere £85,000 in addition, was a native of the town. It was she who, after the death of the king, founded the Benedictine convent in Moret, from which in later years was to come the original and now famous *Sucre d'Orge*—barley sugar.

One note of interest for craftsmen in stone. On the west door of the church, among the sculptured members of its arch, I noticed a spiral fluting which with the exception of a single stone is uniform in its course. It would seem that the mason had miscalculated the flow of his lines and that only when the stones came to be assembled was the error discovered. It may have cost him a sleepless night but little more: nothing daunted, on one small unit of the curve he carved a sharp kink in the pattern and so brought the ends together.

In the late afternoon of the following day I made my way back to St. Mammes. I found that Madame *la patronne* had washed my towel which she had thought needed attention, and as I was going on board again Monsieur presented me with a cheese-box of his *pâté maison*. I moved downstream till I was clear of odorous breezes, and then above a high sandy bank, deeply undercut by the recent flood, I spread my blankets. I was just dropping off to sleep when a sudden whistle of wind in my ear brought me back to consciousness. It was the sniff of a huge yellow ox, the first of a long procession of kine who were as consistent in their curiosity as they were varied in their colouring. I wouldn't have minded one social call, but a series of visitations throughout the night became trying.

Shortly before dawn a band of lemon light appeared on the eastern horizon, and then a blood-red sheen. The light increased, not steadily, but as if thin veils were lifted, one by one. Five herons passed overhead on heavy wings and then a skein of ducks in urgent flight. The flame in the sky gave way to mottled grey and blue. A lavender mist hung over the water as I dipped my oars.

# CHAPTER SIXTEEN

THAT lavender haze above the water was typical of many dawns; again and again the sun would rise through opalescent mists and the water wear its gossamer shroud. But the veils of morning and evening have little to offer to the wood-engraver, however generous they may be to the painter. In engraving one needs precision of form and contrasts of light and shade, for the limitations of the medium are as severe concerning variations of tone as they are austere concerning fluency of line. I incline to think that one of the earliest and most important lessons to be learnt by any art student is the recognition of those qualities most suited to his particular medium, or alternatively of the medium most suited to the qualities he wishes to express. Constantly I see amateurs trying to render in water-colours a subject needing the strength of oils, or attempting in oils the delicacy of the other medium. I was once compelled to refuse a commission for a stone carving from a patron of the arts for no other reason than that the subject he insisted on could only have been carried out in bronze.

It was midday when I came in sight of the plage at Thomery. Here among the dazzle of sunlit parasols and awnings were subjects for many artists: form for the sculptor, line for the engraver, colour for the painter. Most of the ladies wore "Bikinis"—the pointilliste technique might well have been appropriate.

In contrast to present-day bathing fashions, Madame de Motteville in her *Mémoires* has a charming description of Louis XIV and his mother bathing in the river near Fontainebleau. "The King who was still a child," she writes, "bathed also, as well as his tutor, le Maréchal de Villeroy, who never left him for a moment. The queen and all those who had the honour to be with her wore long trailing shirts of grey stuff, likewise the maréchal and his ward, so that modesty was in no way offended." A pretty picture, the maréchal and the boy king in trailing shirts splashing among the queen and her ladies of honour who were likewise accoutred. We are told that the ladies much enjoyed their bathing, and almost every day came from the palace at Fontainebleau to spend hours in the water.

In my little blue boat I dodged a string of barges drawn by a powerful tug. When the last of the vessels had passed the diving-boards were out of sight. The river now was wider and more shelterless than ever, and I had lost my hat—my beautiful palm-frond hat, given to me on Manihiki atoll, ten degrees south of the equator. High in the crown and wide in the brim, it had been woven by some old woman for her chief and he had passed it on to me. Some light air must have lifted it from the boat and cast it on the water. Was it the loss of my Polynesian hat, I wonder, that reminded me of a man I had met in the Pacific? He had come to Tahiti to get away from the rush of modern life in America, and he had married a girl of the island. The longer he lived in his pandanus-thatched house on the edge of the lagoon the happier he was, and the more determined he became never to live anywhere else. But one day business affairs compelled him to pay a short visit to New York, and with him he took his wife. She was enchanted. Never had she dreamt of such marvels as she saw in reality before her eyes. To go back to the Islands seemed to her like going back to a prison from which she had been set free. And all the time her husband could think of little except the day when he would be sailing again through the Golden Gate at San Francisco on the mail boat bound for Papeete. When they reached Tahiti she was more than ever sure that she wanted to live among the skyscrapers; he was equally sure that he could be happy only under the palms. So they compromised, agreeing to spend year and year about in the city and on the island. And all the time they were in New York the American was yearning for the Islands, and all the time they were in Tahiti the island girl was yearning for America.

Thick woods on the left bank heralded the Forest of Fontainebleau, and after a wide bend of the river the bridge at Valvins hove in sight— *le pont de Valvins* where Mallarmé would go of an evening to smoke a cigar and meditate. "It is like a veranda to my house," he used to say.

The poet loved every glade in the forest; every sandy path, soft as moleskin to the feet; every carpet of crisp leaves, studded in springtime with white anemones and violets, or pierced by the croziered fronds of bracken. Through the network of green he would see the luminous stems of the beeches, mottled as the limbs of dryads. Perhaps in his walks he would surprise a wild boar at its rootings, or seeing the flicker of a fallen leaf might watch the questing of a field-mouse. The forest was to him a study and a garden. "Every man has a homeland with its memories of childhood," he said, "and there he hopes to spend his last days. But I have none, therefore I have chosen Valvins."

Mallarmé's house was next door to what is now called *Aux Rosiers*, a small hotel of which Monsieur Marcel Martin is *patron*. I had stayed there before so I knew what to expect: generosity in the bar, temptation at the table, and at the end of the week the account, if asked for, with half the items forgotten. It reminded me of Robert Louis Stevenson's description of Siron's hotel at Barbizon, on the other side of the forest. "It was managed upon easy principle," he wrote. "At any hour of the night, when you returned from wandering in the forest, you went to the billiard-room and helped yourself to liquors, or descended to the cellar and returned laden with beer or wine. The Sirons were all locked in slumber; there was none to check your inroads; only at the week's end a computation was made, the gross sum was divided, and a varying share set down to every lodger's name under the rubric: *estrats*. Upon the more long-suffering the larger tax was levied; and your bill lengthened in a direct proportion to the easiness of your disposition... Your bill was never offered you until you asked for it; and if you were out of luck's way, you might depart for where you pleased and leave it pending."

Nowadays that hotel, under a different name, has a uniformed commissionaire waiting to take tips for opening or shutting the door of your car, and throughout the main street of the once quiet village you find every possible exploitation of the dead artists and their work. The houses of Millet, Rousseau, Diaz, can all be visited at a price. As I passed the Bar l'Angelus, I pondered on the money brought to *other* people by artists, even a century after their death. But then the earthly abodes of saints in heaven have also made good investments, most of them after a much longer interval.

André Billy in his *Beaux Jours de Barbizon* has some pleasant things to say of those artists and poets of the forest. Millet, tall and corpulent, with a long brown beard and the neck of a bull, reading the Bible to his family each evening but postponing the baptism of his children, of whom there were nine, until two or three could be dealt with at the same time. "It costs me less," he said. Could it have been this economy in the purchase of grace that brought about the downfall of one of his family, in the second generation? In 1935 Jean Charles Millet was convicted of forging his grandfather's signature on drawings and paintings of his own manufacture, and was sentenced to six months' imprisonment and a heavy fine. It was estimated that with the help of a friend he had issued between three and four thousand forgeries. It reminds one of the saying that Corot during his life had painted five thousand pictures, of which seven thousand are in America.

Corot, Daumier, Edmond and Jules de Goncourt, Alfred Stevens and a host of lesser known artists and writers stayed "chez Siron," including Murger, the author of *Scènes de la Vie de Bohème.* "We know," says Billy, "that Murger was a writer of the twenty-fifth order, but everyone still reads him." I have an idea that they will go on reading him. Spontaneous, hilarious, robust yet tender, his song of student life in Paris may at times border on burlesque, but burlesque is often illuminating. Who will not sympathize with the playwright, Rudolphe, whose only possessions were his good humour and an oft-rejected manuscript, whose landlord "exhaled a pestilent odour of bad brandy and unpaid rent," and who for a while "lodged in the Avenue de St. Cloud, the third tree on the left as you leave the Bois de Boulogne and the fifth branch." There are few readers who will not envy the musician Schaunard his power of argument with creditors; there are still fewer who will not love Phemie, Mimi and Musette.

Each year from Easter until St. Martin's Day Jean François Millet slept in the open. He knew the healing properties of plants and so achieved a reputation as a "wise-man." With Théodore Rousseau he would make long excursions into the forest. "Le silence, la solitude— Rousseau loves them even more than I do," he said. In the forest Rousseau would sit on a rock for hours, looking into space, lost in thought. "He does not paint," said Millet, "he contemplates. He allows his beloved trees to enter slowly and deeply into his soul. C'est un homme fort, que Rousseau!"

Monsieur Billy tells too of Lantara, a painter who in his early days had been a shepherd and whose memory is still kept alive in the forest by an ancient oak-tree rising from a drift of rocks, "le Dortoir de Lantara." After a long illness, and while still comparatively young, he lay dying in hospital. "You are happy, my son," said the priest to him, "you are on your way to see God face to face for all eternity."

"What, Father?" asked the dying artist. "Always face to face? Never in profile?"

About the year 1830 the idea came to the village tailor at Barbizon, Monsieur Ganne, whose wife kept a small grocery shop, that merely by hanging a sprig of juniper over their door they could promote the business to the status of a tavern. The old barn adjoining the house would make a fine dining-room, and what matter if the swallows did nest under the tiles? Soon, through every window of his house could be seen easels, canvases, pots of brushes and feminine underwear, and in the big dining-room a notice on the wall: "Under penalty of a fine, visitors are forbidden to annoy the artists." "Gaiety, youth and love reigned in the village. What songs and anecdotes! And the glasses that were emptied and the pipes that were smoked. Above all, the discussions on Art and Poetry." As to Siron's, there was no worry about cash. For ordinary clients the charge was four francs a day, but for artists such as Diaz it was two francs seventy. Rousseau arrived there one day still owing three hundred and seventy-five francs from his last visit. He lived there over four months, making one payment of a hundred francs on account during his stay. Then on leaving he borrowed fifty francs to take him to Paris. But the next year he paid the bill in full.

Steps from the water's edge lead under an archway of roses to the shaded *terrasse* at *Aux Rosiers*. There in fine weather all meals are served, and from there one looks across the river to a hillside of cascading branches. At Valvins the peace of growing things is dominant over all: one sleeps in the heart of the forest. As I crossed the narrow road that separates this quiet garden from the hotel, Monsieur Martin came to greet me. He was carrying the corpse of a duck sewn up in a white cloth, its head dangling loose. After telling me that I had arrived at just the right time for his *Ballatine de Canard*, he led me into the bar, put the duck down on the counter and poured me a "glass of welcome." Then picking up his duck again he explained that having taken out all the bones he had stuffed the carcass with its own liver and gizzard, some veal and some pork, all finely minced, along with eggs, onions, truffles and spices, white wine and a little cognac. After that he had stitched it up in the cloth, and now he was going to put it to stew in a pot of bouillon. Tomorrow we would eat it cold for déjeuner.

Madame Martin, who reaches to my elbow and is perky as a chaffinch, came from the kitchen smiling. How long was I staying? she asked. I could have the same room again, the one overlooking the river.

I hadn't really intended to sleep at the hotel, but it was getting late and the sky was loading up with milky-grey clouds. Milk at sunset, water at dawn, I thought. Better stay ashore and have a drop of wine.

I asked Monsieur Martin if my belongings would be safe in the shed in his yard. "I'm the only thief in this district," he said.

Drops of rain were already falling, and as I gave my rope an extra hitch to the mooring post the two house girls came rushing to clear the tables that had been laid for dinner by the river.

Two women, one of them French and the other English, were sitting in the bar when I got back. But yes, the Frenchwoman had been to London. She had been to the Galerie Nationale and she had visited Hampton Court and got lost in the labyrinth.

"The Maze," corrected the Englishwoman.

"Maze?" queried her companion.

"Yes, m-a-i-s-e," said the English lady.

A builder's assistant came in with lime on his face and boots and ordered a glass of red wine. The butcher's boy came in with blood-stained apron and ordered a glass of white wine. Neither stayed more than a few minutes.

The weather was setting in wet sooner than I had expected. I was glad that I was in shelter.

Three workmen came in, wearing blue jeans. One of them, the shortest of the three, with bright red cheeks and well-coloured nose, was horrified when I told him what one would pay in England for the same *vin ordinaire*. His companions laughed at his gestures: he liked the "bons vins" too much, they said, and that was what made his stomach "malade." He said it was better that his stomach should be "malade" and himself happy than that his stomach should "marche bien" and he be "malheureux."

A large car drew up at the door and an American emerged with a portable wireless set. He brought the set into the bar, put it on a table and turned it on full. I looked at the sky but there was no sign of a break.

A little later I climbed to my room and sat awhile watching the rain. Straight as the stems of poplars it was coming down, bouncing like silver marbles on the road, leaping like globules of mercury from the river.

# CHAPTER SEVENTEEN

YES, I had been at Valvins before: in winter when, after a light fall of snow, the secret farings of many a shy creature were disclosed; in spring when chestnut buds were bursting through their sticky sheaths. Now in high summer I came back to another fall of snow, a veritable smother of pure white mayflies. After a few days of intense heat, the evening air was thick with them. Doors and windows had to be kept shut and towels put to every crevice to prevent their entry. They fluttered against the windows and the glass of the doors and fell in thousands. Soon there were drifts of them on every sill and step. Lights in the garden shone through a mist of wings.

"La manne," Madame Martin called them. "They come like the manna from heaven," she exclaimed. But she didn't seem to think that there was anything celestial about them: on the contrary, they were anything but a welcome visitation and when they lay rotting they smelt of bad fish. She had often seen them six inches deep in the garden. They rose from the water after great heat, she said, sometimes for several evenings in succession, and like moths they were attracted by the lights.

I knew that they rose from the water, but I didn't agree with her that they and the moths are *attracted* by light. Why should creatures whose habit of life is crepuscular or nocturnal be drawn to that very quality which their whole nature seeks to avoid? Surely it is dazzle that controls their movements. Once in the rays they cannot see beyond them. Motorists know how rabbits and hares when caught in the glare of headlamps are unable to escape from the light and will often even charge directly at the approaching car. Any salmon poacher will tell you that when once you've got a fish in the beam of your torch it is easy enough to guide him towards the bank.

Only an hour or two of shimmering loveliness in the upper air for these ephemeridae, after two years of uncouth immaturity in the river's mud—the larvae dig small tunnels for themselves in the banks below the water level. A nuptial flight, a laying of the eggs upon the water and then no more.

The forest is so calm, so friendly. Men work there as unobtrusively as woodpeckers. Almost every part of a felled tree is carried away, the remaining scraps of brushwood are burned and their ashes scattered as fertilizer; a pile of trimmed logs becomes as much a part of the life of the forest as the diggings of a mole or badger. Cultivation is by natural regeneration, the saplings are allowed to grow where they germinate; there are no regiments of trees in review order.

I inquired of two woodcutters if they ever saw any of *les sangliers*, the wild boars. One of them laughed. "Demandez à Baptiste," he said, pointing to his companion. Baptiste wasn't very communicative at first—I felt there had been some joke on the subject at his expense—but after a bit of chat among the three of us I learned that towards evening one winter's day, when the snow was on the ground, he had gone out with his gun thinking to follow the track of a boar, and that coming on the animal very much sooner than he expected he had fired hurriedly and failed to touch a vital spot. The boar turned and charged, and Baptiste, missing completely with his second barrel, had just time to jump at the lower branch of a tree and swing himself out of line of the attack. Then he managed to pull himself higher into the branches and climb to comparative safety. But the animal was relentless—they always are when wounded. As darkness fell it was still at the foot of the tree, butting and grunting, and there it stayed all night. What with fear and cold Baptiste was just about unconscious next morning when a search party found him and gave the animal its *coup de grâce*.

"Since then he has never fired at anything bigger than a mole," said his friend.

When a family of *sangliers* is moving through the forest, they told me, it is the female who leads. The male follows her, and the youngsters follow him in line. If they are disturbed they will always try to slip away; it is only when wounded that they become dangerous.

In the last few months of her life, Katherine Mansfield sought health in the forest. She had become a pupil of Georges Gurdjieff, theosopher and psychiatrist, whose *Institut de développement physique, mental et moral de l'homme* was at Basses Loges, about a mile from Valvins on the other side of the river. The purpose of the institute appears to have been to provide a setting for the intensive practice of self-observation in order to develop will-power, and it seems that one of the cardinal principles of Gurdjieff's treatment was to induce in his pupils a state of exhaustion and irritation. To one not steeped in the esoteric knowledge of Turkestan, Afghanistan, Baluchistan, Tibet and China, as this Russian-born philosopher claimed to be, it would not appear to have been the best treatment for a girl in a state of advanced tuberculosis. But it may well be that in her case a more gentle regime was ordained. We know, for example, that part of her treatment was to inhale the breath of cows. In a letter dated 2nd November 1922, she wrote: "Gurdjieff is going to build a high couch in the stable where I may sit and inhale their breath." A little more than a month later, she told how the project had come into being, "It's simply too lovely. There is a small steep staircase to a little railed-off gallery above the cows. On the little gallery are divans covered with Persian carpets (only two divans). But the whitewashed walls and ceiling have been decorated most exquisitely in what looks like a Persian pattern of yellow, red and blue by Mr. Salzmann. Flowers, little birds, butterflies and a spreading tree with animals on the branches, even a hippopotamus... all done with the most *real art*—a little masterpiece... There I go every day to lie and later I am going to sleep there. It's very warm. One has the most happy feelings listening to the beasts and looking."

On 17<sup>th</sup> December she recorded that Mr. Gurdjieff had come to her gallery and talked with her a little: first about cows and then about the monkey he had bought and was going to have trained to clean the cows. Then, nine days later, on the 26<sup>th</sup>, she wrote: "Our cowshed has become enriched with two goats and two love-birds. The goats are very lovely as they lie in the straw or so delicately dance towards each other, butting gently with their heads... I had been talking before to a man here whose passion is astrology and he had just written the signs of the Zodiac on the whitewashed stable door. Then we went up to the little gallery and drunk Koumiss." Less than three weeks later Katherine was dead.

The priory at which Gurdjieff held court had been founded early in the fourteenth century as a refuge for the poor and a shelter for travellers against the dangers of wolves and highwaymen. Later it became a convent, and we hear of Louis XIV and his mother, Anne of Austria, going there "to make their devotions." Madame de Maintenon, one of Louis's later mistresses, who was convinced that she had been sent by God to save the king's soul, also went there to pray.

Under Gurdjieff's rule the feasts, of which there were many, are almost comparable with those of Louis Quatorze at Versailles. Anything up to twenty-five toasts were drunk in vodka or Armagnac—for men the rule was not more than three toasts to a glass, for women six were permitted. There was champagne also for anyone who was thirsty. Gurdjieff maintained that he had so many patients passing through his hands that he was compelled to *see* them as quickly as possible, and he found that by inviting them to dinner and plying them with liquor he could the more quickly penetrate their reserve. At these dinners, "what hors d'oeuvres, what caviare, what fish smoked to strange colours, what pigeons stewed in vine leaves, what hams of bear's flesh! And the rose and poppy sweetmeats, and the Turkish delight!" After dinner, exotic "religious" dances were performed before the arch priest who sat cross-legged on his dais.

There are many who, having known him personally, believe that in spite of his eccentricities he was not less than a prophet. Others who stayed at the institute thought differently, and one at least, a man of letters, found "signs of hooves and horns all over the place."

Earlier letters of Katherine Mansfield tell of the intensity with which she identified herself as a writer with her subject. Of her story *The Voyage* she relates: "When I wrote that little story I felt that I was on that very boat, going down those stairs, smelling the smell of the saloon. And when the stewardess came in and said, 'We're rather empty, we may pitch a little,' I can't believe that my sofa did not pitch... It was so vivid—terribly vivid... It wasn't a memory of a real experience. It was a kind of *possession*." In another letter she says: "I have just finished a story with a canary for the hero, and almost feel I have lived in a cage and pecked a piece of chickweed myself."

So often people ask an author how it is that he finds the exact word, *le mot juste*, to convey his thought. The answer was given by Carlyle: "Poetic creation, what is this but seeing the thing sufficiently? The *word* that will describe the thing follows of itself from such clear intense sight of the thing." More recently Somerset Maugham has written: "It is not enough for an author to see a thing with his eyes, he must apprehend it with his nerves, his heart, his bowels." In art it is the same: Hokusai, one of the greatest of Japanese artists, told his pupils: "If you want to draw a monkey you must *be* a monkey." Poussin, one of the greatest of French painters, remarked: "There are two ways of seeing things; one is simply looking at them, the other means considering them attentively." An author must identify himself utterly with his subject: even if he is a teetotaller he must, when describing conviviality, feel blithe as Omar; even if he turns the scales at twenty stone he must, when writing of the ballet, feel light on his feet as Lopokova.

Added to such intensities, there is for the author an urgency in "getting things down" while they are still vivid in his brain. Life passes with such kaleidoscopic changes that unless a word, a thought, a phrase, is recorded almost as it is born, it is lost. That at any rate is my experience. It is no good saying to myself, I'll write that down in the morning. By next morning it is gone for ever.

Here I will confess to a little bit of play-acting on my part which has got me over a few such difficulties in Ireland. With the stories flying fast and furious of an evening, the only thing I could do was to develop "a bit of weakness," or maybe "a chill." This would necessitate hurried exits from the scene of poetic narrative. "Sorry, boys," I'd say, with my hand to my waistline, "I'll be back in a minute. Don't tell another story till I come back," I'd say, and then I'd rush upstairs to my room and scribble like mad. And after I had come down again and there had been another good story, I'd rush off once more. "My God, isn't the poor fellow bad?" I'd hear them saying as I hurried off. And then when I'd returned a second time, there'd be a glass of whisky waiting for me. "Throw it back in you now, man—'twill do you good, boy," they'd say, and maybe they'd ask me was it from sitting in the wet I'd got taken bad, or from sleeping out in the boat?

There is the same need for intense analysis and immediate recording in drawing or painting. A note made during the first ferment of perception has qualities not easily recaptured. One is rarely given a second chance.

# CHAPTER EIGHTEEN

ONE evening in the bar at *Aux Rosiers* I heard a story which I was assured had local origin, but which like many another tale so described might well have come from a good many other places. It concerned a ventriloquist who, while staying in the Fontainebleau district, met a peasant who was grazing his donkey at the side of the road.

"That's a fine ass of yours," said the ventriloquist.

"He's getting old," said the peasant.

"But he must be a valuable animal," said the ventriloquist.

"He'd be worth a thousand francs," said the owner.

"A thousand francs? Why, man, an animal that can speak like yours is worth a hundred thousand francs. Listen to him," he said. And with that came a voice from the ass on the other side of the road, telling of the succulent flavour of the thistles he'd found there.

The owner was mystified.

Further conversation ensued in which the ass took a leading part.

"Why, if he's worth all that," thought the owner, "I'd better sell him." So as they were on the road to Fontainebleau and it was a Friday and market-day he drove the donkey into the town. Needless to say all he got for his pains was laughter, for once parted from the trickster the animal refused to speak.

A sad story, but it reminded me of a happier one I had come across a little earlier in my travels. It is common to many parts of France, with variations, and because it might just as easily have come from County Cork I have transmogrified it into the Anglo-Irish idiom and called it, "The Perfect Wife."

Once upon a time there was a man by the name of Timmy O'Riordan who, along with his wife Mary Kate, lived in a small cottage in the country.

"Timmy," said she to him one day, "we're poor, and it looks to me we'll stay poor unless the one or the other of us does something about it. Why wouldn't you do like Paddy Mac beyond and drive a few bargains? He's at it all the time and his pockets are busting."

"How would I drive a bargain?" asked Timmy, who had never done more in his life than follow horses on a farm.

"Easy enough, man. 'Tis only to change what you have for what you haven't."

"Maybe I'd lose in the deal, and what would you say then?" said Timmy.

"Did I ever utter a hard word to you whatever you did?" said Mary. "Look here," says she, "we have the pig. Take him along with you and do a little bit of a trade with him."

So Timmy tied a bit of rope to a hind leg of the pig and drove the animal before him down the road. He hadn't gone far before he met a man with an old nanny goat.

"Where are ye off to, Timmy?"

"I'm going bargaining."

"And with what are ye trading?"

"The pig, to be sure."

"Don't go another step. Take the goat instead."

"'Tis a deal," said Timmy. And with that he handed over the pig and went on his way with the goat.

"Where are you going, Timmy?" asked a man who carried a goose in a sack over his shoulder.

"Bargaining," said Timmy. "I gave the old pig for the goat."

"Faith, you must keep that up. Would you change the goat for a fine goose?"

"I would," said Timmy, and off he went with the goose. Before no time at all he had changed the goose for a barn-door cock; and then as he reached the town he saw an old woman scraping up manure from the road.

"Would you make much of a day with that, ma'am?" he asked.

"Fair enough," says she.

"Would you take a rooster for the bucket full?" he said. "I would," says she.

So Timmy, with his bucket of manure, stood at the street corner wondering what to do next. Who should come up to him but Paddy Mac, his neighbour, the wealthy one.

"Wisha, Timmy," says he, "what are ye doing here?"

"The same as yourself," said Timmy. "Bargaining!"

"And how's trade?" asked Paddy.

"I gave the pig for a goat," said Timmy.

"What'll Mary Kate say to that?"

"She'll agree, to be sure. And I gave the goat for a goose, and the goose for a cock."

"What'll Mary Kate think of that?"

"She'll be delighted, of course. And I changed the cock for this manure."

"D'ye know," said Paddy, "I wouldn't be in your shoes when you get home tonight. You'll have the warm time of it, I'm thinking."

"And why so?" said Timmy. "She'd never argue."

"She will tonight," said Paddy.

"Would you bet on it?" said Timmy.

"I'd bet you ten pounds," said Paddy.

"That's a lot of money," said Timmy.

"Will you take it?" asked Paddy.

Timmy thought awhile. "I will," he said.

So the two of them together went back to Timmy's cottage.

"And how did ye get on?" asked Mary Kate when the two of them appeared at the door.

"Grand," said Timmy. "I changed the pig for a goat."

"Nothing better," said Mary. "We never had enough scraps for the pig."

"But I gave the goat for a goose."

"And weren't you wise, all the same. We wanted a few feathers for the bed."

"But I changed the goose for a cock."

"Better than ever. He'll wake us early. 'Time saved is money won.'"

"But I changed the cock for this manure."

"Well! Aren't you the sensible man? 'Twill be great for the garden."

"Say no more, the one or the other," said Paddy. "Here's the ten pounds. Only one thing I'll say to ye, Timmy, and that is that whatever other trading ye do never exchange herself, for there isn't the likes of her in the whole world."

As he went out at the door Mary Kate turned to her husband. "Isn't it a wonderful price you've brought for the pig?" she said.

May I tell just one more in the same vein, this time from Touraine?

Once upon a time there were three fellows on a journey together, and they came to a small village. "We'll have a drink here," said one of them, pointing to a pub. "We will, and some food too if we can get it," said the others. They'd been travelling all day and were half starved. And when they went inside didn't the woman of the house put as much before them as would feed six. So they ate and they drank and 'twas only when they rose up to go that each remembered that he hadn't a copper on him.

"I'll pay for the lot," said the youngest of the three, fumbling in his pocket.

"To hell with you," said the eldest, "'tis I'll do it."

"Leave it to me," said the third fellow, fumbling too.

In no time at all they were near to fighting.

"For the love of God, will ye quieten yourselves? There's only the one need pay, whoever it is," said the woman of the house.

"Listen here to me," said the eldest of the three to the woman. "'Tis easy enough to decide. Will you put a cloth over your eyes and the first man you touch will pay."

"Fair enough," said she, taking a handkerchief from her apron pocket and tying it across her face.

The knot was hardly fixed before the three men had jumped through the open window. And who should come in at the door at that very moment but her husband?

Blindfold, his wife stretched out her hands and took a grip on him. "'Tis you will pay," says she.

"You never said a truer word," he said, as he took the bandage off her eyes.

# CHAPTER NINETEEN

"WHY not go on to Paris by barge?" suggested Monsieur Martin.

We had had three days of intense heat at Valvins, and I had begun to think that for the next stage of my voyage some other means of locomotion than my small boat must be found. Below Valvins the river would be getting wider and wider, and already the number of doll's-house villas on either side did not encourage intimacy with its banks. I felt that I needed more speed.

"How could I find a barge to take me?" I asked.

"Row down as far as the lock at Samois," said Monsieur Martin, "it is only three kilometres from here. Go ashore there and have a word with Monsieur Boyer at the hotel. He knows all the *mariniers*—he will arrange it for you. Wait," he said, "I will give him *un coup de téléphone.*"

Monsieur Boyer's reply was that it would be a simple matter. He suggested that I should come along next morning and he would arrange everything. But when I reached the lock it was Madame Boyer who came from the little Hôtel de l'Écluse to welcome me. Her husband, she explained, had forgotten when speaking on the telephone that today would be Friday, and every Friday he had to go to the market. But he would soon be back. Was I thinking of leaving my boat in Samois? she asked. If I had no further need of it there was a neighbour who was wanting a fishing punt—perhaps I would sell it to him.

As the day wore on I began to think it might be a wise policy to dispose of the boat in Samois. I wouldn't want it after Paris, and if, as now seemed reasonably sure, I was going to continue my voyage by *péniche* I might just as well let the poor little thing go, however sad I might be at parting. When Monsieur Boyer returned towards two o'clock in the afternoon he confirmed what his wife had said about a purchaser. At five o'clock the same evening, as I stood by the lock gates and watched the new owner, with the blue oars in his hands, rowing towards a backwater where other craft were moored, I felt almost as if I had given away a spaniel.

Just then four barges coming downstream were entering the lock. Might as well start negotiating at once, I thought. I addressed a Hebe who stood on the prow of the leading vessel and inquired if she would like a passenger. She answered "No" most emphatically, adding that she had enough children on board already, whatever she meant by that. I approached the second barge in the convoy, *Yvette* by name, but before speaking to anyone on board I noticed that she had a fresh coat of tar on her, before and behind. *Ariadne*, immediately astern, carried bales of firewood and showed little deck space. *Père Antoine*, the last of the fleet and hardly more than a lighter, was low in the water with cement. It was getting late, and it occurred to me that a night on board any one of them might not reach the heights of luxury; I decided to postpone further parleys until next day. But somewhere about nine o'clock, as I took a bedtime stroll by the river, I noticed a barge moored for the night a short distance above the lock. The skipper, a handsome young man with dark curling hair and bright blue eyes, was coiling a steel cable on the for'ard hatch when I hailed him.

But certainly, he said, he would be delighted. I was welcome. He would be leaving at half past six in the morning, as soon as the lock opened, and he hoped to be in Paris by four in the afternoon. That would depend, of course, on whether we had "la chance" with the locks.

If they were ready for us as we arrived we would make good speed; but if we had to wait while they dealt with the barges coming upstream we might be an hour or so late. He smiled: "C'est la vie des mariniers," he said with a shrug. As I left him I was just able to make out the name in brass letters on the bow; it was the *Robert*!

I went on board next morning as arranged and soon after seven o'clock we passed through the lock. The skipper, by name Robert Cohn, had introduced me to his wife, a splendidly built woman with hair as rich and eyes as bright as his own. I would say there wasn't much between them, either, in physical strength. Yes, Madame told me, they had four children. She added a little apologetically that of course they had only been married a few years.

The barge was about a hundred and twenty feet in length and loaded with sand and gravel. The two holds made nice play-pens for the children. Midway between the holds were the two-roomed living quarters. Astern, the wheel-house was bare of all furniture save a high stool for the helmsman and a small table.

No sooner were we through that first lock than Madame disappeared down the hatch amidships. I thought she had gone to inspect the children who as yet had made no appearance, but a cloud of black smoke that belched from the stack pipe and blew aft into our faces hinted of other activities. It wasn't long before she emerged bringing with her, along the narrow cat-walk of a deck, a large jar of black coffee and a bottle of rum. Then she took the wheel while her husband and I refreshed ourselves.

Madame went for'ard again, leaving Monsieur and myself to agree upon the relative virtues of that elixir from Martinique, Jamaica or the Guianas. The morning was cold and misty and we were glad of the comfort. Some inhabitants of a camping-site on our left were tramping and stamping in the dewy grass, waiting for their kettles to boil. We passed a barge from Belgium and then one from Holland.

At our next lock Madame went ashore with shopping bags, and before the water was down she was on board again, heavily laden with provisions. It generally takes about half an hour to get through each lock, and there is always a Café de l'Écluse where necessaries can be purchased. At the small locks of the upper reaches, little but wine and beer and Vichy water seemed called for to supply the needs of mariners, and a give-and-take system existed by which one could hand back the empties at any lock where one took on fresh supplies. But in these sophisticated waters the cafés had developed into veritable stores, where the barge wives could do all their household shopping. As the tall gates closed behind us and we swung into the open river once more, we had another tot of rum. The day was brightening.

The country above the lock had been flat and featureless; now it became hilly and wooded, with strange oddments of pink-and-white match-box architecture dotted among the trees. It was getting towards nine o'clock and, as we moved along, a child's head, highly polished, appeared in the hatchway, to stare a moment at the apparition that had come aboard. That was the eldest of the family, said Monsieur Cohn. He would be four years old in September. A quarter of an hour later a girl's head appeared and disappeared. That was number two: she would be three in October. After another short interval the mother lifted the third child to see the stranger, but it became alarmed and was taken below hurriedly. I did not see the infant. It was still in the cradle.

With the children dressed, Madame turned her attention once more to the wheel-house. This time she brought along a tray of biscuits that she had purchased when ashore. I opened a bottle of red wine that I had brought with me. The day was getting warmer.

Madame went back to her offspring—"Jamais tranquille," she said. Her husband remarked that barge life was a fine one for the children—plenty of fresh air and freedom. I couldn't see a great deal of freedom in such cramped quarters—even less so when Madame returned to the wheel-house with three of the children and put them sitting on the table beside me.

At Melun, a town famous for its eels, we passed close to the high walls of the prison with armed guards watching from their observation turrets at each corner, then through the intricate rafters of a temporary wooden bridge and, soon after, under a rippling network of reflected light that played on the new and graceful arc of concrete which spans the river.

Below the town the country on either side of the river was park-like with isolated oak-trees giving shade to cattle. Madame was now on deck standing over a wash-tub that she had balanced on a plank across the hold. Her splashings were lost in the sand below. When, half an hour later, she emptied the tub over the side, there were enough children's pants on the line to make any father proud.

We had passed through several locks but at each "la chance" had compelled us to wait till upriver traffic was cleared. Because of these delays we found ourselves again and again in the same company, tied alongside the *Paul Émile*, the *Riga*, or the *Hero* in the basin of the lock, the slower moving craft having had time to catch up with those of greater horse-power.

On one stretch of river our engine gave a few moments' trouble and forced us to slow down. Almost immediately the *Paul Émile*, a short way ahead, slackened speed and waited for us. Then, as if automatically, a cable was thrown and we were taken in tow. As we approached the next lock the cable was shortened and adjusted so that the two of us lay side by side; a second line was thrown to hold the sterns together, and together as a single stately unit we passed through the gates with not a hand-span of clearance on either side. It seemed to me a pretty note of etiquette that, because we had been the first of the line at Samois in the morning, pride of place was accorded to us throughout the day.

The children had now lost their shyness and were scrambling on the floor of the wheel-house among my legs and those of the table. It seemed rather a small space for five people. I went outside and stood on the narrow deck for a while, but Monsieur called me back to point out an ancient barge that was being towed by two lean mules and a horse. He said it had come all the way from the Midi. I suggested that it was heavy work for the animals. At one time it had been done by men, he replied, even by women and children—many a child had died of it. But that kind of thing was all over now.

During my absence the children had been playing with my hat. I noticed that the youngest of them had a nasty rash on her head. The weather was getting a bit oppressive, I thought.

Shortly after noon Madame came astern to say that déjeuner was ready. She took the wheel while Monsieur and I went for'ard to a fine lunch of rabbit and green peas. When we came back it was the children's turn. Their mother took them away, and the air seemed cooler.

Unlike most of the barges we carried neither dog nor cat, not even a tortoise such as I had seen on one deck—perhaps there was thought to be sufficient life on board already. But the cabin was as gay as a gipsy wagon with crockery and bright chintz. Nearly all the barges have pots of growing flowers, and seldom do the elder children miss a chance to jump ashore and gather posies of wild ones.

I remarked to Monsieur that higher up the river I had noticed barges travelling on Sundays the same as on any other day of the week.

"Every day of the year they travel," he said, "except 1st May and 11th November."

I knew that 1st May was Labour Day, but for the moment I had forgotten about 11th November. "What saint's day is that?" I asked.

"La fête de St. Armistice," he said, laughing.

I have it on the authority of a French professor that the modern word "corbillard," meaning a hearse, derives from the very slow river ferry that once plied between Paris and the town of Corbeil, which lies some dozen miles below Melun. I have it on the authority of an encyclopaedia that the first stand for public conveyances in Paris, during the seventeenth century, was outside the Hôtel de St. Fiacre. The cabs very soon became known by the name of the saint, and the coachmen adopted him as their patron. But you can't be sure of anything in this world, no matter how good your authority. I was told many times by an English professor, a Fellow of many learned societies, that the only music worth hearing was that of John Sebastian Bach; and then quite by chance one evening, near a bandstand in a park, I saw him kissing a she-professor while the band played Strauss. But perhaps he wasn't listening.

St. Fiacre is also the patron of gardeners. Soon after he came to France from Ireland he settled near Meaux, a town some twenty-five miles north of Melun, and there beside a chapel he enclosed for himself a garden. And we are told that such was the work of his hands and the zeal of his religious devotion that his garden was in no wise affected by the rigours of the seasons, and God gave him always of the fruits of the earth an abundance. And he built there a hostel and gave welcome to rich and poor alike; but it was always with fear that he saw the approach of a woman, having it ever in his thoughts that it was by her that man had lost his soul. The fame of Fiacre spread throughout the province until it came to the ears of the governor who then, wishing to honour the holy man, came with his wife to visit him. And the wife, seeing the radiance of the saint, was overcome with a shameful desire for him. Day and night she thought only of her guilty craving. Thus driven, she came again to the garden and begged of the hermit that he would take her with him in flight.

Astounded and aghast the saint recoiled from her, taking refuge in his chapel and praying to God for grace. She then, with jealous anger raging in her heart, hastened to her husband and, blind to all truth, made accusation of the holy man. He had wished to despoil her of her honour which as her husband well knew, she said, was more to her than her life. Upon this the governor, wounded and grieved beyond measure, sent messengers to lay hold upon Fiacre and bring him before him, and the woman, not content with her vile calumny, and desirous only to heap further humiliation upon the saint, went with the messengers. But at the very gate of the garden God struck her and she fell dead. Then the governor knew that she had lied, and he made atonement with the saint.

Fiacre lived for many years after until God called him, but through the years no woman ever again durst approach the garden lest she be smitten with pains and torments. After his death the garden received his name and the fruits thereof were distributed in abundance to the poor.

In view of the saint's natural antipathy to women, it is strange to relate that in the village of St. Fiacre there is today in the church a stone known as the arm-chair of St. Fiacre in which, by sitting skin to stone, sterile women may achieve the blessing they desire.

The town of Corbeil shows little of distinction from the river. Large flour-mills are there in plenty and fleets of barges are moored on either bank waiting to take the produce to Paris. Here we left behind us the barges that had been our companions during the day. For the rest of the journey we travelled alone. Madame, having removed the children's garments from the line, had become busy with a tub of heavier clothes. Later she came and removed the children themselves from our company that she might repolish their faces. Monsieur pointed out to me a place where his barge had been sunk by enemy fire during the war. Three times he had suffered machine-gunning from their aeroplanes.

It was after seven o'clock when, behind a trellis of cranes, gantries and factory chimneys, we saw the Eiffel Tower in a golden haze. At Choisy-le-Roi, a suburb of Paris, our journey came to an end. We tied up to a quay where huge cones of sand and gravel awaited our quota. Another biscuit, another glass, and we parted as members of a family.

# CHAPTER TWENTY

AT a luncheon given in London during the spring of 1952 by Miss Christina Foyle, in honour of Augustus John's book, *Chiaroscuro*, one of the speakers, Mr. T. W. Earp, remarked that when a man sits for his portrait to a great painter it is inevitable that in so doing he should lose something of his identity. "Popes have become Titians," he said; "kings have become Velasquez." And then, referring to his own portrait by the artist whom we were honouring, he said: "Even an Earp becomes a John."

Something of the same transformation occurs with landscape painting. Often during my voyage on the Seine I had seen stretches of the river as Monets or Renoirs, and that evening after I had left the barge, and as I made my way through the suburbs of Paris towards Montparnasse, I saw the streets only as Utrillos. How that artist loved the texture of old plaster! How those white walls of his teem with colour—calm and restful, strange product of a tortured mind. Eight litres of wine he would drink—nearly two gallons—before reaching the state of mental exaltation necessary to his work. But had he not had his *vin rouge* we should not now have our Utrillos.

In Number Three gallery of the Musée d'Art Moderne, a small octagonal room, hang sixteen paintings, eight of them by Utrillo, eight by his mother, Suzanne Valadon. Her life history is as colourful as that of her son. While still a child she had come from the neighbourhood of Limoges to Paris where, attracted by circus life, she began to train as an acrobat. But a fall from a trapeze caused injuries which put an end to her prospects in that profession, and she became a model. She posed for Puvis de Chavannes, Degas, Lautrec, Renoir and others, and it was while working in their studios that she herself began to paint. And then in 1883 when she was eighteen there happened what has been called her "second accident": unmarried, she gave birth to a child. It was a happy accident for the world of art, for the child was Maurice Utrillo.

The identity of the boy's father is doubtful—even his mother seemed uncertain—but it is probable that he was an amateur painter named Boissy, a drunkard born of a drunkard father. This may well explain the chronic alcoholism which attacked Maurice even in his schooldays and dominated the most important and the most prolific years of his life as an artist. By 1921 he had entered asylums of one kind and another eight times in search of a cure. It was at the age of eighteen, after the first of these visits, that his mother, wishing to divert his thoughts, put brushes and colours into his hands. Thereafter, his life became "a rhythm of drunkenness and the painting of a daily masterpiece." The streets of Paris, and above all of Montmartre where he and his mother lived, supplied his subjects—the cafés, the churches and the windmills. Those streets and squares were his favourite scenery, his habitual companions, for a morbid temperament shut him off from friendship with fellow artists. At times when his mental state was such that Suzanne locked him into a room on the upper storey, he would go on painting from memory with the aid of the picture postcards which she gave him; at other times, maddened by the desire for drink, he would leap from the window and escape again into those streets. Yet in one year he completed 150 canvases.

In 1909, when Suzanne was forty-four and Utrillo twenty-six, they exhibited together at the Salon d'Automne, each for the first time. In the catalogue for that year we find their names one below the other: Utrillo (Maurice), *Pont Notre-Dame*; Valadon (Suzanne), *Été*. But it was not till 1919 that Utrillo's work began to attract public attention. Until then you could have bought a painting of his for a few francs in almost any junk shop in Montmartre, where, as often as not, he had exchanged it for a litre of wine. From then onwards the prices of his canvases mounted steadily. Suzanne died in 1938. She had had to wait longer than her son for success, but before her death her landscapes, her nudes and her still lifes, with their vigour of design, line and colour, had given her an assured position.

Robert Coughlan, in his recent short but trenchant biography *The Wine of Genius*, completes the picture of Utrillo's life. In 1935 the artist married a widow, a lady of strong personality and decided views who, after Suzanne's death, settled him in a villa of "confectioner's pink stucco" in a rich suburb of Paris. There, surrounded by life-like ceramics of frogs and turtles, an aviary of parakeets and a dog-run of Pekinese, she established "an ironclad and antiseptic regimen" that varies little as the years pass. He has become a religious addict, a devotee of Joan of Arc, and spends hours each day kneeling in the chapel that has been built for him close to the house. He seldom goes out, and never unattended by a manservant. He still drinks a little but the wine is heavily watered. He still paints a little, occasionally with something of the old quality. Almost always the subject is Montmartre.

Montparnasse in August had a different air from when I was last there. Most of the artists were in the country, and most of the models seemed to have gone with them. Those hard-ups who had been forced to remain behind looked a little parched, a little browned at the edges like the leaves of the plane-trees. Many of the cafés were shut, their pavements bare of chairs and tables. Many of the shops too were celebrating their *fermeture annuelle*. But here and there on the boulevards or in the cafés that remained open one would see a young man carrying a paint-box or a pair of canvases, or a girl who might well be a model. At the Rond Point, where I stopped for an aperitif, a girl with black hair falling to her shoulders was sitting on the *terrasse*, an empty coffee-cup before her. Although the evening was warm she wore a full-length fur coat whose loose collar she adjusted from time to time across a bosom that seemed to have little other covering. Was she another Kiki? I wondered. Kiki, at one time Queen of the Quarter, who considered a raincoat and a few inches of tulle round her neck to be ample clothing when going from studio to studio. A young man with portfolio under his arm stopped for a moment on the pavement before us to light a cigarette. Quickly and imperiously the girl called to him. He obeyed her summons and coming close bowed in greeting. She took his head between her hands and, drawing it towards her, kissed his forehead on both sides, then took the cigarette from his lips and put it between her own. Smiling, he disengaged himself and continued on his way.

Contemporary with Kiki in Montparnasse was Lili in Montmartre, another model with much the same propensities—inside a studio she could not abide clothes. It was she who on one occasion caused some slight embarrassment to my friend Monsieur de Baar, now proprietor of that excellent restaurant in London, Père Auguste. He was a student at the time, living in Montmartre, and among his friends was one Paul, a painter, for whom Lili acted in all the varying capacities of housekeeper, model, etc. De Baar, living alone in his studio, fell ill, and after several days of solitary misery wrote to his mother in the country, telling her of his plight. The following day Paul, hearing of his friend's misfortune, sent Lili along to look after him, and no sooner had she arrived than in a perfectly natural way she discarded her clothes. And then the bell rang. Well, it could only be another artist come to inquire, or perhaps a tradesman looking for payment of his bill—tradesmen were accustomed to studio life. Lili opened the door, and who was outside to confront her but the mother of the sick man. That evening his temperature soared.

What with my long day on the river and the little drops of comfort I was now absorbing, I began to think about dinner. Where would I go?

There are artists and authors who like to sit in overcrowded cafés, hardly able to see beyond their own table with the smoke, hardly able to hear those at their own table with the noise, hardly able to raise a fork without jogging a neighbour's elbow. But give me La Coupole in the Boulevard Montparnasse, where, as the double doors are pulled open for my entrance, I see a table for four being pulled forward for my acceptance. The place has style and that's a thing of importance to an Irishman. A few years ago, when there was a momentary boom in agriculture, half the farmers in County Cork put up magnificent gates to their estates. The fact that the hedges or walls on either side of the gates remained broken down didn't take away from the grandeur; a gap or two would be handy for the straying animals.

There were no gaps or hedges at La Coupole that evening. The *patron*, whose birthday is the same day as my own, greeted me and treated me as an elder twin should greet his junior. We discussed the city of Reims and its amenities. And after dinner, with coffee served by a magnificent dark-skinned gentleman in Turkish dress, I sat outside and watched the life flow by. A seller of newspapers passed among the tables, calling his wares in accents harsh as a corncrake's—"*Paris-Presse, Paris-Presse! France-Soir, France-Soir!*" The inevitable vendor of imitation Persian rugs and imitation polar bearskins appeared. A little old woman, grey and wizened, shuffled along offering buttonholes of camellias. And

then a gnome of a man, with pointed beard and deep-set eyes, came up and whispered something to a stout man with a bald head who sat at the table immediately in front of mine. The big man thought a moment, pursed his lips, lifted his hands and shrugged his shoulders, but said nothing. The gnome slunk away. What long story lay behind that brief episode? I wondered.

Light from the cafés spilled in pools on to the pavement and climbed the mottled trunks of the plane-trees. As the night grew late, colours deepened: the black of hats, of coats, of taxis, grew more intense; the henna of a woman's hair, the yellow of a poster, shone more luminous. Negroes' faces became lost in the shadows, the pallor of white faces was turned to flame in the neon lights.

As I bade good night to the *patron* and was about to say a word in praise of his cuisine, I heard an English voice: "Things aren't the same at home now. In the old days, when we had the manure from the horses, everything tasted different. Didn't it?"

# CHAPTER TWENTY-ONE

On Sunday mornings the boulevards of Montparnasse are almost deserted. Inside the cafés there is scarcely a client; outside the chairs are piled on the terraces. As I walked towards the "Select" for my morning coffee a man with a long broom was sweeping the pavements. He paused a moment and, bending down, opened a stopcock which released a stream of water into the gutter. The water sparkled over innumerable gleaming coins, the tops of mineral-water bottles which café waiters habitually flick off, into the gutters. An occasional figure hurried along carrying a bottle of milk or a bâton of bread. Only at the corner of the Boulevard Raspail was there any organized activity; there the artists were erecting their screens and hanging their pictures for the day's exhibition. And close behind them, at the corner of the Rue Delambre, the copper-haired flower seller was arranging her blossoms. The colours under her canopy were deep and rich; crimson and scarlet gladioli; bunches of tight little dahlias, magenta and lemon; closely folded rose-buds. She was tying up a bouquet of red, white and blue— an outer ring of scarlet carnations, then a ring of white ones, and a centre of deep blue cornflowers. In England we try to make our cut flowers look "natural" in their vases; the French prefer to treat each blossom as a unit in a formalized scheme of decoration. In England we treat Guardsmen on ceremonial parade in just that way—as units of decoration.

Later in the morning I strolled among the statues in the gardens of the Tuileries. A pair of pigeons cooed to each other from the heads of

Adam and Eve as they fled from Eden. A young man deep in thought, regretful or ambitious, sat solitary in the shade of Pan. At the foot of a plinth whereon a mighty tussle was taking place between nymph and faun, a lady with knitting in her hands was gently dreaming. On the seats or on chairs drawn close, in poses as intimate as those of many of the carvings, couples were making and breaking promises. And through this constellation of statuary, dead and alive, girls, comely as Renoirs, were pushing prams that held other people's babies. Then on a lawn, amid flower-beds rich in scarlet and gold, I saw an old man almost hidden in a foam of fluttering wings. The pigeons clustered on his head and shoulders, on his arms and feet; they even clung to the pockets of his jacket. He had a number of small sacks of different colours from which he would extract grain, and the grass around him was completely obscured by feeding birds. At intervals, as if following some secret rhythm, he would dance almost on tiptoe to another corner of the garden where the birds, after a wide circling of the aerial stage, would group themselves around him once more, like feathered Sylphides. When disturbed by a passing stranger they would rise as a fountain into the air, spread wide like spray, and drop again to earth.

From the Tuileries I made my way eastwards, passing the great arch set up to commemorate the victory of Napoleon in 1805, and found myself in the Place du Carrousel where nearly three centuries ago Louis XIV offered to his queen, the princesses and his friend Mademoiselle de La Vallière the most sumptuous fête that French eyes had ever beheld. Louis was interested in all things theatrical and was himself an excellent dancer. It was at his court that ballet as we know it today came into being—which is the reason why so much of its terminology is in French. This pageant was ostensibly to celebrate the birth of the Dauphin, but its real purpose was the solemn affirmation of vast political ambitions. Louis appeared before his people in the costume of a Roman emperor, showing himself as "the living chalice of Monarchy": he would destroy the power of Austria and Spain, and build again the empire of Charlemagne. His tunic for the occasion was of silver brocade embroidered with gold; large diamonds were set in the gold. His collar carried forty-four clusters of diamonds, his epaulettes were as richly adorned. His threefold sash was decorated with a hundred and twenty rosettes of diamonds, of exceptional size. His helmet with scarlet plumes was of silver and gold and showed no lack of gems; its chin-strap alone carried twelve rosettes. His scimitar was so encrusted with diamonds that it was difficult to see the gold in which they were set. Even the cream-coloured horse on which he rode was second only to himself in the glory of its trappings.

The future did not materialize entirely as "le Roi Soleil" had foreseen it, but no doubt Mademoiselle de La Vallière enjoyed the party, and, before she was superseded by her friend Madame la Marquise de Montespan and went into a convent, may well have worn some of those stones.

There was no pageantry that day as I walked through the *place*, only a few sparrows spattered on the gravel and a woman on excruciatingly high heels leading a white poodle trimmed in the latest absurd style. Isn't the clipping of these animals the last insult to the canine race? Of all dogs the poodle is the most intelligent. It can be trained to do almost anything, from telling the time by a clock to smuggling. One of them, owned by a shoeblack whose pitch was by the Pont Neuf, was taught to splash the footwear of passers-by in order to increase his master's trade. The poodle is a splendid water dog—in fact its French name, *caniche*, is derived from its prowess with duck shooters. Even if its hair tends to grow long and need clipping, that is no reason why the dog should be turned into a clown and made an object of ridicule.

I passed under an archway of the Louvre and reached the quay. Enough of walking, I thought, as an empty taxi came towards me. "To the Trocadero," I said, "le Musée de l'Homme." Arrived there, I had my lunch on the veranda. Behind me was a tall totem pole from British Columbia; before me the Eiffel Tower, almost a totem to Parisians. And when I had reflected on totems and taboos, the *carte des vins* and the menu, I made my way upstairs to the galleries. I suppose it was the *ballet des colombes* of the morning that brought me to a first halt before a feather cloak once worn by an Inca chief. Gaudy and glorious, three broad horizontal bands of red, yellow and blue feathers attached to an underlying fabric; it was hard to believe that it was not one of the many feathered cloaks brought back from Hawaii and Tahiti by early travellers in the Pacific. Thor Heyerdahl, in his book *American Indians in the*

*Pacific*, since published, uses this affinity among many others to emphasize his argument that the original inhabitants of Polynesia came from the Americas.

Feathers again. Now I was looking at a copy of a Bushman's wall painting—four black-and-white male ostriches and two grey females arranged in as neat and lively a composition as one could wish. A bird approaching from the right is arousing something more than interest in the others. Although the three birds nearest to him are moving away they have their heads turned in his direction and are watching him with suspicion. The remaining two who have reached a safer distance have turned completely about and seem prepared to be aggressive. It was only after I had been looking at the drawing for some time that I noticed that the intruder had the legs of a man and, almost hidden, an arm which held a bow. The design is a happy composition but it is also a valuable record of a method of hunting among the bushmen of Rhodesia. The same people when following larger game such as the elephant or rhinoceros will camouflage themselves under the head and hide of a hartebeest, imitating the actions of that animal as they move through the long grass towards their quarry.

From feathers to eggs, hens' eggs decorated with the most intricate patterns in many colours. It is, or was till recently, the custom in many parts of Europe for young people to give these to each other as presents on Easter Sunday. A whole case in the museum is devoted to examples from Lithuania, Poland, Czechoslovakia, Hungary, Rumania and

Russia. It seems that before ornamentation is begun, the eggs are either hard-boiled or blown and then filled with wax, the latter treatment of course giving greater permanency. One method of decoration is to dip the egg in a bath of dye and, when it has taken an even stain, work on it with the point of a knife in a manner similar to modern practice on scraper-board. The result is a tracery of white on a monochrome background. More elaborate patterns in a greater variety of colour are obtained by a process akin to Javanese batik. In this the eggs are given varying applications of wax before successive immersions in different dyes, until eventually designs of the most astonishing intricacy are achieved. It is the custom then to have the eggs blessed in church and afterwards to exchange them among friends. Doubtless few who take part in the ceremonies know or care that the giving of these eggs is the relic of a Jewish custom that was adopted from the religious rites of the ancient Egyptians and Persians, and that the egg has been for thousands of years a symbol of resurrection.

I pondered on these things as I sat in the Métro on my way back to Montparnasse, and I remembered the painted eggs that on Easter morning in Ireland would be hidden for us children by our parents. It was no more strange then to find an egg with stripes of red and green on it under an inverted flowerpot than it is today to find a mallard's nest within sight of the Horse Guards Parade. It is ever a source of wonder to me that to watch at close range some of the shyest of our wild birds we have to sit by a pool in the heart of London.

Time passes quickly in Paris. I think it was about two evenings later that, after dining in the Place St. Michel, I wandered along the quay towards Notre-Dame. The cathedral was floodlit, ivory white against a purple sky. The glare of the lamps threw into clear relief the traceries of walls and windows, cast ghostly shadows among the many buttresses. Suddenly behind the colonnade between the towers there showed a golden arc. As quickly as it had appeared it climbed until, a perfect sphere, the moon hung high in the heavens behind the tall shadowed spire. Normally one thinks of moonlight as silver and cold, but that night it was golden and warm. Glowing and alive, it moved upwards through the sky: the church beneath it was ashen white, immobile, built as it were of dry bones. It was no longer a solid structure; it seemed a façade, a skeleton of itself painted on a dark backcloth. Overhead the moon rose higher and higher in the firmament. It poured its gold into the river, and the lamps on the bridges added faint echoes to its lustre. Lovers under the arches ceased a moment from their embracing; *clochards* turned on their hard beds and glanced upwards, while in the street above them from all the moving traffic heads craned to glimpse this giant sunflower of the night.

## CHAPTER TWENTY-TWO

INSTEAD of feathers it was plaster casts that hit me in the eye when I visited the Musée d'Art Historique, twin building to the Musée de l'Homme on the Trocadero hill. A whole wing of the building is devoted to reproductions of early ecclesiastical sculpture. It was difficult to believe that they were of plaster and not stone. As I was to learn later, many of them were very much easier to study in those well-lit gallery aisles than in the comparative obscurity of their churches. Even the great exteriors of doorways lost nothing by their change of setting.

It has been said that the French have always known how to flavour serious thinking with the spice of humour, and here I found the truth of that statement exemplified in many lively instances, notably on the *tympan* of the west door of the thirteenth-century cathedral at Bourges. The subject is the Last Judgment. St. Michael in the centre, with a pair of scales, weighs a chalice against an imp of hell. On his right the elect simper their way towards the bosom of Abraham; on his left the damned are being pitchforked towards the cauldron of hell by demons with winged rumps and gargoyled bellies. In the cauldron the central figure is a lady who, to add to her discomfort, is having one of her breasts devoured by a toad. Her only companion in the pot is a tonsured monk whose tongue suffers the same misfortune. But they will not be alone for long: two bishops in their mitres, and nothing else, are about to be thrown in head first, and two more tonsured brothers are on the way to join them.

But it was the earlier work, that of the eleventh and twelfth centuries, that was to me the most impressive. During that period of history France was recovering from the invasions of the barbarians and her artists were rediscovering the potentialities of stone. Times of exploration in a new method of expression are always the most vital: the discovery of fresh possibilities in a medium is stimulating to the imagination. It is only when all possibilities have been determined that art tends to become academic. Everyone then knows the grammar of his language even if he has nothing to say.

Next morning I bought a ticket for Autun and hopped into an appropriate train. How comfortable a French train can be, how comforting the *wagon restaurant*! I expressed my appreciation to a man who shared my table.

"Ah, monsieur," he said with an air of great wisdom, "the English do not complain. They will accept whatever is served to them. If they would only complain they would get a better cuisine."

I had in my pocket a copy of a book which told of the travels in France of Lord Blayney. "They weren't always so uncomplaining," I said as I opened it and showed him this extract from the diary of the noble lord, noted at Tours on 12th March 1811: "I had a party to dinner this day, but all my rhetoric was insufficient to prevail on my landlady to serve it *à l'anglaise*; that is, to give the fish and vegetables as part of the first course. Her obstinacy so put me out of temper, that to her great astonishment and mortification I threw the whole of the first course, consisting entirely of French dishes, out of the window, dishes included; and ordering up the second, we made a tolerable dinner of it." Alas, my fellow traveller's English was weak: he could not appreciate the full flavour of the narrative.

Just then the steward came to ask if we would take a liqueur—cognac, benedictine, cointreau, crème de menthe? My companion interrupted: he would like an Armagnac and nothing else. And so some minutes later the steward returned and we had two Armagnacs poured for us, as if we were twin Dukes of Gascony.

On the day of my visit the great façade at Autun suffered from two disadvantages: that it faces into a narrow street and that it acted as a sounding board to the wireless which blasted from one of the open windows on the other side of the street. It was from the steps of this very church that in 1487 the threat of anathema on the slugs had been proclaimed. I wished that another threat at nearer neighbours could have been published that day.

On the great tympanum of stone immediately above the double doors of the church the figure of Christ in glory dominates all else. The subject, as at Bourges, is the Last Judgment, but it is an infinitely finer rendering. On the right of Christ stands a group of the chosen, among them St. Peter, who, holding an enormous key, directs an angel who is lifting one of the blessed into the first arcade of heaven. On the left of Christ, St. Michael and Satan are weighing souls in the balance, and demons thrust the damned into the jaws of hell. There are some ninety figures in all, of which nearly half are on the lintel and form a frieze at the foot of the central figure. These are the dead rising from their coffins and on their way to judgment. Already one of them has been seized from above by a mighty pair of hands and, doubled up with fright, is about to be hoisted towards the scales. Here, too, a husband turns to hold his wife's hand in sympathy; pilgrims in hope of indulgence display the insignia of their journeyings to the Holy Land and Spain. A monk who has managed to preserve his habit from corruption is one of the few who are clothed.

The figures are graded in size according to their importance: that of Christ is many times larger than any of the others, the saints are taller than the angels, the angels than the men and women. Yet there is no feeling of incongruity; the size, like the pose, of every figure seems inevitable: one cannot think of any alternative, one could not wish for any alternative. I remarked to a priest who came from the building that whereas in the reproduction in Paris the head of Christ was missing, here on the doorway the figure was complete.

"It is only a few years since the head was found," he said. "The models were made before that time." Then he told me how towards the end of the eighteenth century taste in art was such that the authorities had caused the whole tympanum to be concealed under a layer of bricks and plaster. In carrying out their orders the workmen, finding that the protruding head of Christ complicated their work, broke it off at the neck and threw it away. The plastering was removed in 1837, but it was only in 1948 that the head was found and replaced. It had been lying throughout the century among some other stones in a cellar.

Inside the cathedral one finds endless delight in the capitals of the columns. They have all the naïveté, humour and vitality that one so often finds in children's drawings. On one of them an angel of the nativity is appearing to the three Magi who, under the one rich quilt and wearing their priestly crowns, lie together in the same bed. With one hand the angel points to a star, with the other he touches lightly the hand of the nearest Wise Man. The touch has awakened him, his eyes are open; the other two are still asleep. On another pillar Noah's Ark is perched on the top of Mount Ararat; Noah looks out of an upper window, two animals peer with surprise from a lower opening; on one side grown-up sons are unloading provisions, on the other Noah's wife is disembarking some younger children.

Among other biblical subjects are Shadrach, Meshach, and Abednego in the fiery furnace; the flames surround them but the spirit of God in the form of a dove hovers above them. On another capital Simon the Magician takes a terrible toss on to the point of his chin, between St. Peter and a goat-headed fiend from hell. There is also, of course, a Nativity and a Temptation.

But as on other churches of the Middle Ages, secular subjects are not prohibited. A cock-fight, a man dancing with a bear, a dwarf fighting a gigantic bird, Androcles and the lion and many strange devices of monsters find their places in the sacred buildings. Such subjects came in no way amiss to the medieval craftsman. On the *tympan* of the church of St. Ursin at Bourges are scenes from the fables of Aesop who lived about the sixth century before Christ, and in the church at Mas-d'Agenais in the Garonne district there is a representation of a whale dragging to destruction a shipload of mariners who, mistaking the creature for an island, had moored their vessel to its side. This, as many will remember, is one of the earliest adventures of Sindbad the Sailor, as related in *The Arabian Nights*. Here it is meant to demonstrate the wiles of the devil. Even more surprising as a means of inculcating virtue are carvings found on ancient churches, here and there about the country, which if exhibited today anywhere but on a sacred building would lead inevitably to altercation with the law. Time, gentle mediator, has cast a veil of modesty over some strange imaginings.

In my hotel that evening was a man who said he had business in Nevers next day. He was going there by car and I could have a seat with him if I wished. There was a cathedral in that town also, not as fine a one as at Autun and he had heard it had suffered in the war, but if I was interested, well, I was welcome to the lift. It would be as easy for me to get back to Paris from there as from Autun.

He was a thick-set little man with close-cropped grizzled hair, a tuft of dark hair above the razor line on each cheek, and several long black hairs growing from the tip of his nose. His eyes were very blue. His face and his hands had the tan of old sunburn. He spoke a little English. I got the impression that he was a sailor come ashore. In this I proved right. When we shared a table at dinner and were offered langouste he was emphatic in his refusal. That was something he could *not* eat: he had seen too many of them. He told me that though he now lived in Dijon, he was a Breton and came from Camaret near Brest; his father had been connected with the fishing industry in that part of Brittany, owning a number of the boats and having shares in others. He himself had been to sea many times, in the boats that went to the west coast of Ireland after the langouste. He enjoyed those trips to Ireland; sometimes they would take bottles of brandy with them and smuggle them ashore—

there were plenty of caves where they could be hidden, but it was easier to sink a few of them in a lobster-pot with a special mark on the buoy: then their friends could pull them up when they pleased. He thought that that western part of Ireland, near Galway, was very like Finistère. There were the same whitewashed cottages with thatched roofs, and the same small black cattle. The people, too, were *sympathique* with the Bretons. He was very proud to be a Breton: they were a different people from the French. I thought of the story of an Irishman who, in the last century, lay dying in London. He was a descendant of one of the many Protestant English settlers who during the reign of Elizabeth I had been "planted" in Bandon, Dunmanway and other southern towns in Ireland. Unlike most of his kind he had not been "assimilated." They brought an Irish clergyman to see him.

"I think you're Irish like myself," said the visitor to the dying man.

"I'm no Irishman," came the reply. "I'm from Bandon."

"And isn't Bandon in Ireland?"

"The Israelites were four hundred years in Egypt but they weren't Egyptians," said the man in the bed.

As we left Autun next morning, I got a fit of sneezing—any few grains of dust will set me off.

My companion began to laugh. "Why do you do that?" he asked. "I am not dead, and there is no *tabac*." Then he told me that on one visit to Ireland he had been taken to a wake. "I went inside to the cottage," he said, "and it was full of men and women. Some of the women was kneeling by the bed, and some of them was sitting on the chairs, and many of the men was holding glasses in their hands. And the man that was dead, he was very old, he was lying on the bed in a new *complet* of clothes, and on his chest there was a plate with some *tabac*—I think you call snuff. And then Monsieur Gorman who bring me to the party he take a pinch of the *tabac* and he tell me do that also, and then we put it to our noses and then we sneeze. But I could not stop the sneezing! I sneeze and I sneeze and I sneeze. And they give me a glass with some whisky, but when I hold it in my hand it spill each time when I sneeze. It was terrible, and so I have to run away, and I do not go back because of all the smoke that was in the room. In the morning my eyes was more red than the eyes of the men who had stayed there all the night."

His happiest recollection of County Galway was of an evening in another cottage, when a couple of boys, having hidden a creel of lobsters under a settle, let the creatures loose at an opportune moment. It was at one of the usual Saturday night gatherings of neighbours for dance and song and story-telling, and the lads persuaded an old man to tell the story of a girl who, the night before her wedding, had been taken by the sea-women and kept at the bottom of the ocean until her lover gave back a ring of gold that he had pulled up on his fishing-hook. There was only the fire to light the room, and just when the old man was telling of the slimy strands of weed that reached up around the girl, and the hundreds of outstretched eyes that would be watching her day and night, and the claws that were for ever holding her prisoner, the girls on the other side of the room saw firelit stalked eyes probing the darkness and a multitude of claws groping their way towards them. There was a screeching and a yelling, and the boys added to the joke by jumping on to the chairs and the table as if they too were terrified. The only one present who was in no way perturbed was the woman of the house who, having two cauldrons of water on the fire for boiling clothes, picked out the shirts and pants and as quickly put an end to the threats of the unfortunate lobsters.

I asked my Breton friend why he had forsaken the Atlantic and was now living in the middle of France. He replied that a few years ago an uncle of his had died and left him an interest in the *fabrication de pain d'épices*. Spiced bread was, of course, a speciality of Dijon, and his firm there kept to the old recipe of wheaten flour, honey and the yolks of eggs, with aniseed and other spices. But he could not remain inland any longer. Indeed, it was because he had had one offer for his business from a firm in Autun and another from a firm in Nevers that he was now on the road. One day soon he hoped to be smelling the tar on the boats instead of the tar on the roads. He wanted his children to be brought up among boat-builders and not among bakers. Instead of playing in the streets, they would have all the run of the beaches. At Camaret they could still watch men shaping the planks with an adze and cutting the beams with a long handsaw, one of the sawyers standing in a pit below and getting all the sawdust in his eyes. That's the advantage of being "top sawyer," I thought.

When we reached Nevers I said good-bye to my companion and made my way to the cathedral. Alas, it was far from being what I had expected to see. Disaster had indeed befallen it during the war. Its roof had been destroyed, its walls blasted, its windows shattered—the leading of their glass hung in the empty sockets, twisted as windblown cobwebs. On the ground, close against the outside of the ruin, lay fragments of carved pillars like knucklebones, scraps of arches, mouldings, altars. Inside even some of the foundations had been laid bare.

But they were rebuilding. Work had been going on for eighteen months. They thought that it would need another four or five years of it before completion. The activity was exciting. There seemed to be, again, the zest of medieval building. In the courtyard apprentices were sawing through five-ton blocks of stone fresh from the quarries; in the nave masons were cutting mouldings. A foreman was setting out the units of a Roman arch on the floor; renewals for a Gothic window lay ready, marked and numbered for assembly. Baulks of timber for buttresses were there. In one of the chapels a carver was putting the finishing touches to a capstone. On the pavement before the broken altar men were mixing mortar. Shovels scraped on the floor, hammers rang on steel chisels. Everywhere in the aisles and cloisters there was zeal: men like ants clearing and repairing their trodden galleries.

# CHAPTER TWENTY-THREE

M<small>Y</small> friend Alan Bott in London had offered me a trip in his motor vessel, the *Yarvic*. "Any time you like," he said. "Up the Seine or down the Seine, or across the Channel, or all three if you prefer. She sails Paris-London once a fortnight and carries Pan books. I get some of them printed in France. You can sleep in the hold with the books or share the captain's cabin—please yourself."

So a few days after my return to Paris from Nevers, finding a letter for me with more precise details of the ship's voyaging, I took a stroll along the Quai de Gennevilliers, and there I saw her in the new little harbour with the top of her mast just showing above pier level. The skipper, Captain Peters, emerged from the wheel-house and looked up at me. An athletic young man, tall, with dark hair and a short beard, he was wearing a navy-blue blazer with brass buttons. "H'm—ex-R.N.," I thought.

He welcomed me aboard with R.N. hospitality. No, he wasn't R.N., he said as we chatted.

"R.N.V.R.?" I suggested.

"Just out of the army," he said. "Going back to Cambridge in October—history. Oh well, you know, everyone takes that. You've only got to mug up medieval Germany."

"And your navigation?" I asked. "Where did you get that?"

"In the desert," he replied with a smile. "Spent six months there, soldiering."

The *Yarvic* had been built during the war for carrying ammunition to warships in harbour; when that service was no longer needed she found another vocation. In the course of time some thirty feet had been added to her length, but before her figure had been altered and while she was still less than seventy feet over-all, she had occasion one misty evening to hail the liner *Queen Elizabeth*, 83,000 tons. "What ship?" she asked.

"*Queen Elizabeth*," came the reply, "and you?"

"M.V. *Yarvic*."

"Thank you—thought you were a buoy."

A pretty wit, these Elizabeths. It is told that when for the first time she of the white ensign passed her sister of the red in mid ocean, the signal from the battleship read "S N A P."

In the wheel-house, which was also the lounge, the ship's office and the dining-saloon, it was resolved that I should sign on as a supernumerary member of the crew, with the understanding that my duties would be negligible and my pay less. I remembered when once before I had signed on on those terms. It was for a voyage on a coaling tramp between Sunderland and Barcelona, and the sheets on my bunk were the same as those of the last two passengers, without intermediate changes of air. That was a remarkable voyage if only in this respect, that when we left Sunderland there was a small chunk of coke resting on the starboard gunwale, and so smooth was the sea even in the Bay of Biscay that when we tied up alongside the quay at Barcelona that biscuit-light fragment was still on its narrow perch. Incidentally, the same applied to the half-inch of coal dust on my cabin floor, but a gale wouldn't have shifted that. It had been trodden by so many feet that it had the consistency of a sorbo mat. This time, on the *Yarvic*, everything was spick, span, and spotless. I had only to come aboard on the morrow half an hour before sailing time, I was told, and an arm-chair would be awaiting me. Orient Line and P. & O. might have more elaborate decorations in their saloon—after all they have more room for them— but they couldn't have better springs in their chairs.

Next morning on the quay, by the bollard above the *Yarvic*, I bowed to a gentleman as he was about to put a foot on the first rung of the ladder leading vertically to Captain Peters' bridge. Immediately he withdrew his foot and bowed to me, insisting that I should take precedence in going aboard. Yet somehow in a way known only to pilots he landed on the deck at the same time as myself. Monsieur *le pilote* was jovial and full of talk, in a mixture of French and English.

Normally when a ship is leaving port there is a certain amount of commotion both on board and ashore. Gangways have to be raised, thousands of feet of paper ribbon have to be thrown, orders must be shouted through megaphones; but when the *Yarvic* sailed there was nothing of that. On board all was calm; ashore no one paid the slightest attention. The pilot had taken off his new jacket and hung it on a peg behind the wheel; he had pulled on a pair of overall cotton trousers so patched with varying shades of blue that it was difficult to decide which was the original garment and which its repairs. As he adjusted the safety-pin that did duty for a top button the captain gave a quiet order to stand by. There was a moment's delay as the safety-pin broke loose and needed readjusting; then the pilot assumed command. A few casual words and we had cast off, some action on the part of the engine-room staff and, behold, we were moving, slowly and silently, out of the harbour and into the main stream of the Seine.

Slim, the chief engineer and mate, whose name belied his figure, moved with speed and suddenness. If at one moment he was spread-eagled on a bunk or a hatch, his head thrown back, his eyes closed as if in sleep, at the next he might be bent double as if in pain over his latest thriller. Slim is a philosopher. A laugh is his first answer to any problem, pleasant or unpleasant. If the anchor chain stuck and a kick from his heavy clogs appeared to be the only remedy, a cheerful bellow was the prelude to his rush along the deck. Gale warnings got a similar reception. Zealous harbour masters were listened to and then laughed at until they laughed themselves. But he was ever alive to anything that affected the ship. Even when asleep at night it seemed he could keep count of the ships that passed us on the river.

On board the *Yarvic* there were no complications of modern seafaring in the way of speaking-tubes, telephones, etc. A double stamp on the iron floor of the wheel-house with a well-shod heel was sufficient to call attention from galley or engine-room, immediately below. Nor did food reach the bridge by electric lift or uniformed steward; a hole in the floor gave perfect access from the galley. The fact that the hole was under the pilot's seat insured against accidents to both limbs and crockery. Rowden the cook had learned his job from a former captain who had shown him how to poach an egg; since then he had relied on his own inspiration. Tilly the bosun wore his peaked cap with an air of distinction: it was the only sign of uniform on the ship. The remainder of the crew—a boy named Pullen, Canadian by birth—could speak French. All of this I was to learn during the days ahead.

Now we were leaving factory chimneys behind, and wide meadows spread on either side: beyond them on the left bank the forest of St. Germain, its château hidden in the trees.

Traffic on this part of the river was very much heavier than it had been above Paris. Long strings of barges towed by their tugs were moving up and downstream. In these sophisticated waters the kilometres from Paris are clearly marked on the river bank. Here too I found a variation in the etiquette of river travel as I had known it: when entering a lock, we as a seagoing ship flying the priority flag of a gold crown on dark blue took precedence over all single barges, but all convoys of barges, and they were many, took precedence over us. Thus it was that as we approached our first lock, at Bourgival, we gave way to a muster of six barges with their tug, watching them pass us and slip into their places inside the gates, two by two, demurely as choir-boys, before we took our own modest place in the last available corner.

There is always time to stretch your legs ashore while the water in a lock is going down. It was a warm day, and I had thought of a glass of beer while the skipper was buying bread and fruit, but four representatives of the barges were already in the café when I entered and they invited me to join them in their bottle of Beaujolais. They were lamenting that it was difficult to get good cheese in Normandy, all the good Camemberts were being exported to England. The only ones in France nowadays that were good, they said, were those that had been re-imported from England. I told them that in one of the best hotels in Beaune, the centre of the Burgundy wine trade, the majority of the wines offered were of the year 1940, one of the poorest vintages on record, whereas those of '45, '47 and '49, all excellent years, did not appear on the wine list. They looked at each other sadly, raising eyebrows, hands and shoulders in a simultaneous fatalistic gesture. In England people speak with their mouths, but in France they express themselves with every limb and feature except their ears.

One of the company looked outside and said that the water was down. "C'est plat," he said. But when we went outside, we found that it wasn't yet quite "plat," so we returned to the counter and split another bottle, this time on me. Where did I come from? they asked. "Cork," I told them. "Oh, but you have a great hero for the liberty," said one, "MacSwiney, the man the English let die." Then they inquired if I liked Beaujolais, and when I replied that I did one of the party began to sing. It was a verse from an old Burgundian drinking song:

Quand je suis las et solitaire,
Fatigué par un long chemin,
J'aime, dans l'ombre et le mystère,
A m'isoler le verre en main.

When I am tired and without friends,
Weary from the day's long road,
I like, in some quiet shaded place,
To sit alone, my glass in hand.

But before he had got any further with his song there was a shout from outside and we all hurried to our ships.

I think it was Pascal who wrote, "Rivers are roads which move and which carry us whither we desire to go." The gates of the lock opened, and the Seine carried us onward towards the sea. At Confians Ste.

Honorine we found battalions of barges drawn up in ranks on both sides of the river, many of them just arrived from or on their way to Belgium and Holland by way of the Oise, which joins the Seine below the town.

"L'église des mariniers," said the pilot, pointing to a cream-coloured barge with comparatively high upper structure. "It is a church both for the Catholics and for the Protestants. It is a school, too, for the children of the barge men; but they do not have much time there."

We passed a group of eight barges gay with flags and bunting. One could hardly see their outlines through the maze of decoration. "Les noces," said the pilot. He picked up the megaphone and shouted to them: "Mes hommages à vos amours!" But the wedding party must have been celebrating on shore, for we had no reply.

The Oise is "Stevenson's river." It was between Vadencourt, above Origny, and Pontoise that he made the latter part of his *Inland Voyage*. More than once he was unfortunate in his choice of hotels, and speaks of one as "of cursed memory"; but were he to return to that valley today he would forget all delinquencies on seeing the devastation that has since befallen it.

On re-reading the narrative of his journey after I had completed my own adventurings on the Seine, I was amused to find that he too had started in a flood, he too had seen his canoe whirled as a leaf in the current, he too had had to swim. But, whatever its hurry for the sea, his river did at least keep within its banks, whereas mine had had no sense at all. He could when he wished go ashore and bestow his limbs in a meadow; there were days on end when I hadn't seen a blade of grass.

All the time moving quietly forward—how easy it is when you have an engine astern, an engine whose power needs to be curbed rather than encouraged. The river hereabouts was studded with islands. As we approached Villennes I noticed that all the crew had come on deck. Slim came into the wheel-house and appropriated the binoculars. "Nudist colony on that island," he said.

"Never seen anything yet," said the captain.

"Never know your luck," said Slim.

We passed the island, heavily embowered with trees and shrubs. No sign of human life was visible.

"Tantalisant," said Monsieur *le pilote*.

# CHAPTER TWENTY-FOUR

THE river shone silver under silver clouds. In its wide sweeps it had acquired a new majesty. The gold of corn stooks stippled its banks; the emerald of new clover fields shone as jewels in the landscape. Tall white sails of pleasure craft moved like phantoms among the low, heavily laden barges. Then in the hillside near Mantes a mighty chasm carved in the cream-and-white chalk, and around it the roofs and chimneys of cement works, deeply blanketed in dust with great grey cones of debris rising in their midst—a lunar landscape.

"'Mantes la Jolie!' Voici une ville qui a beaucoup souffert," said the pilot as we passed under another of the new and graceful concrete bridges. Two thousand bombs had been dropped on the town during the last war, he told me, first by the enemy, then by the Allies.

"Mantes la Jolie": the adjective was first applied early in the twelfth century when, after being completely destroyed by William the Conqueror, the town had risen again, literally, from its ashes. In the year 1087 William, annoyed by the raids of neighbouring chieftains into his Norman territory, demanded possession of the towns of Pontoise, Chaumont and Mantes. When this was refused he entered Mantes and, sparing only the château, destroyed every other building. Then it was that, while he was admiring his work of annihilation, his horse stumbled and he was thrown, grievously wounded by the pommel of his saddle. They carried him dying to Rouen and there, repenting that in his destruction of Mantes he had not spared the church of Notre-Dame, he bequeathed sufficient funds for its rebuilding, and died soon after.

Such was William's death. Of his birth the story is a happier one. It seems that one day in the town of Falaise, Duke Robert of Normandy when passing a stream that ran near his castle noticed a girl kneeling at her scrubbing-board, with sleeves uprolled, washing clothes, even as today one may see women by almost any stream in France. He was told her name was Arlette, and that she was a daughter of Fulbert the tanner. That evening a messenger from the duke came to Fulbert asking that his daughter should be sent to the castle. Our reflections today on such curt wooing might be critical had we not evidence of Arlette's subsequent response. In an ancient chronicle we read that "at Falaise a town of Normandy this Duke Robert fell deeply in love with a girl by name Arlet daughter of a certain pelterer, and she, when she was led to the duke's bed, tore her nightgown from chin to feet, and, asked why she did this, replied that it was neither lawful nor permitted that the lower part of the gown which went round her feet should now turn to the face of her lord. And by her the duke begat a son by the name of the Bastard afterwards Conqueror of England. And she falling asleep dreamed that a tree came out of her womb which overshadowed all Normandy."

From other chroniclers we learn that this meeting, far from being a mere episode in the emotional life of the duke, was the beginning of a love that lasted until his death. "He cleaved to her alone and loved her as his wife." Nor was he unmindful of her family; her brother was raised to high office, her father was created Ducal Chamberlain. It is as pretty a story as one could find in a fairy-tale. If we wonder why a marriage was never celebrated the answer is that at that period of Norman history the princely line paid little attention to the canonical laws of matrimony, preferring what was known as "*mariage à la Danoise*"—the Norse invaders dispensed with formalities on such occasions.

After Duke Robert had died in the Holy Land, Arlette married one Herluin de Conteville, by whom she bore a son, Odo, who was to become the famous Bishop of Bayeux. As the Catholic Encyclopaedia tells us, "the life of this prelate was scarcely that of a churchman. He even had a son, called John." Odo helped his half-brother William to prepare for the Norman invasion of England and despite his profession fought in full armour at the battle of Hastings, salving his conscience by using a mere mace instead of a sword. 'Tis wonderful what acrobatics ecclesiastical consciences could perform in those days. There was the same Duke Robert's uncle, who was Archbishop of Rouen. In his episcopal role he was unable to marry, but holding also the lay title of Count of Évreux he was in that capacity able to take to himself a wife and beget children.

Let it not be thought that I object to clerics fighting. If a man believes that the cause is righteous, why not? In Gallipoli in 1915 there was a Catholic padre who, when most of the Munster officers had been killed or wounded, whipped off his badges and led the men in another attack. I don't know what the bishops would have said to him if they had known, but I do know what the surviving Protestants said to him: "We'd go to hell with you, Father."

Whatever may be said of the "fickle and ambitious" Odo, "the slave to fleshly lust, who would never abandon his vain and wanton wickedness," and who, while in England as viceroy of William I, "wrought castles wide amongst the people and poor folk oppressed," historians appear to owe him at least one great debt of gratitude. It is now generally agreed that it is to Odo's initiative that we are indebted for the great strip of embroidery, seventy-seven yards in length, known as the Bayeux tapestry, a document described by Sir Eric Maclagan as "an inexhaustible storehouse of information about the life of the eleventh century." It is believed that it was at Odo's order that the work was carried out in England by needlewomen as skilled in embroidery as English men of the time were skilled in the art of illumination. Incidentally it would seem that Odo himself was not averse to being portrayed in roles of distinction, such as saying grace at a banquet after the landing at Pevensey, or rallying his troops at a critical moment in the fighting.

From an artist's point of view, apart from the information to be gathered concerning arms, armour and articles of dress, it is the grouping of the figures in the tapestry and the vigour of their actions which will most appeal. As on the western façade of Autun cathedral, where a mere eight of the elect can suggest a host of heaven, so in the tapestry at Bayeux a dozen men on horseback can suggest a squadron of cavalry or as few on foot an army of infantry. And for the horses, what magnificent falls, for the men what delightful choppings off of head and limb! Surprising the difference between subjective and objective thinking. I knew an artist who, while coolly and calmly engaged on a most fearsome battle picture with men dead and dying in all directions, pinched his finger in the drawer of his painting cabinet; and the fuss that man made jumping about on the floor of his studio, and the language he used, would have launched a regiment of tanks into battle.

It is strange to think that but for the wise action of a court fool William the Conqueror might never have landed in England. He had not yet reached his twenty-first year when a conspiracy of the Norman barons nearly put an end to his life. William, ignorant of the plot, was visiting his castle at Valognes, in the Cherbourg peninsula, without troops and with only his suite. His jester, Gallet, on leave from the court, was staying in a village some few miles distant from the castle. And by chance the stable in which he was lodging that night belonged to the house in which the barons had assembled. Towards midnight Gallet was awakened by the noise of horses and men in the yard. Peering through a window he saw men in armour: listening, he heard talk of surprising and killing his master. Quickly and quietly he slipped away from the stable, made his way to the castle and gave the alarm. William leapt out of bed, scarcely waited to dress himself, but barefoot, in hose and shirt, mounted a horse and disappeared. Then in the darkness he rode through the same country and close to those very beaches which nine centuries later were to witness an invasion from England to liberate France. Next day by the road that still bears his name, "La-voie-le-duc," he reached the village of Ryes where a loyal vassal not only provided him with a fresh horse and a bodyguard of his own three sons but, when the pursuers arrived, led them on a false trail. Home at Falaise, William, having put his castle in a state of defence, enlisted the help of Henri I of France. Together, on the morning of the 10th August 1047, they met the rebel barons in the Val des Dunes, near Argence, ten miles west of Caen, and routed them in battle.

Most of us carry in our minds but a single picture of past heroes, usually taken from the time when they were at the height of their fame. We would find it difficult to think of Shakespeare with thick hair on his scalp and little on his chin; of Nelson with two arms and both eyes; of Henry VIII without a paunch. It needs a similar effort to visualize the young "Conqueror," galloping through the night, clad only in his underclothes, his ears strained for any sound of his pursuers.

G. G. Coulton in his *Medieval Panorama* recalls a pleasant anecdote concerning William. Writing of St. Hugh of Lincoln and his disputes with Henry II of England, he says: "This pious and bold Bishop of Lincoln had excommunicated the king's chief forester for infringing the liberties of the Church; again, he had refused the king's request for a Lincoln canonry in favour of one of his courtiers who was not ecclesiastically suitable. The king summoned him to Woodstock. Hugh found Henry sitting on the turf in his park, his courtiers in a ring around him. Not a soul rose to greet the bishop, and he realized that this was at the king's bidding. Therefore he 'quietly laid his hands on the shoulders of a great councillor who sat next the king, and made a place for himself at the royal side.' Still there was dead silence. Henry, to show his unconcern, told a courtier to give him a needle and thread, and began to stitch at a bandage on his wounded left finger. At this the bishop remarked, 'How like you are now to your ancestors of Falaise!' an allusion to the fact that William the Conqueror's mother was the daughter of a tanner of Falaise, and in those days leather-dressers were commonly leather-sellers and leather-workers, so that 'the cobbler' may well have become a proverbial nickname. The king, 'struck to the heart by this smooth yet razor-like stroke, clenched his fingers and burst into uncontrollable laughter, rolling over on the ground with his head in the grass and his face in the air; in which posture he long gave way to his laughter without control.' The courtiers, even the most shocked, could not repress a smile. Henry explained the jest: then he turned to Hugh and argued both cases reasonably with him. He found himself wrong on both points and was frankly reconciled."

That evening, the first since Paris, the sky was already lit with stars when the *Yarvic* came alongside an oil barge moored to the bank above the lock at Rolleboise. We had noticed some inviting lights from a restaurant on the waterfront as we drew near. Now it was only a matter of climbing across the deck of our neighbour and clambering up a grassy bank to reach the road and a few minutes later the village. Captain Peters and I performed all three evolutions with alacrity. A warm glow from behind red-and-white check curtains led us to the door of "L'Escale," and from the door the *patron* led us to a table under ancient beams.

# Chapter Twenty-four

"You have come by road?" he asked curiously, having seen no sign of a car.

"No," we said, "by river."

"You have a yacht?" he asked.

"We have *un vaisseau marchand*," said the captain proudly.

"Une péniche?" questioned our host, a little surprised.

"No, not a barge. A *vaisseau* that carries books—and a passenger," he added, bowing towards me.

"Before they made the tunnel through the hill and brought the railway," said the *patron*, "there was a ship which carried eighty-nine passengers. It would come here from Poissy, drawn by four very strong horses. They would go at a trot nearly all the way, along the towpath. Voyagers preferred it much to the *diligence*. It was *plus confortable, moins fatigant*. When the voyagers arrived here there would be two wagons for them—one that would go to Rouen, one that would carry them to Évreux." Yes, he could recommend the Château Duhart-Milon '45—it was a very good wine.

He recommended some very good solids too. When later we joined Slim in the bar we were as comfortable as he was happy.

"Ran way from home, I did," said Slim. "Eight years old. Joined the gipsies at a fair—stayed with 'em till I was fourteen, travelling around. Then went fishing—trawling, for herrings and mackerel in season. Joined the navy when I was seventeen—two years commandos. Got arm bust up—it's all right now. And here I am—*Yarvic*." Slim gave his usual burst of laughter.

Peters and I left him to his private navigation. "That man likes nothing better than to take the helm in a rough sea and nurse the ship as if she were a child," said Peters to me as we walked back to rejoin the *Yarvic*.

# CHAPTER TWENTY-FIVE

Next morning, after we had passed through the loch below Rolleboise and were approaching Vetheuil, we saw on our right the first of the white escarpments which become such a feature of the chalk hills bordering the lower Seine. In the cliffs were many caves, natural and artificial, that have been used by man as habitations for himself and as shelters for his cattle since his earliest appearance in the valley.

"Many people went to live in them during the war because they were safe from the bombs," said the pilot. "Many have stayed there to live since the war. They are warm and very dry." He pointed to a church tower that protruded from a grassy slope. "L'église souterraine," he said. "The church is underneath, it is inside the hill. It was cut out of the rock in the year 1670. You can see the windows in the side of the hill. The roof is round like a barrel."

In a high point of cliff immediately above the church we could see a number of large grottoes. "That is le Grand Colombier, the great dovecote," said the pilot. "There is a room there that is more than one hundred metres in length. It is called *la salle du chef normand.* You will see in it the place of the throne and of the big oven with the sides of tiles, and of the fire-place with holes in the walls for *les ustensiles de cuisine.* It was the home of a great Norman chief. There are many other dwellings in the cliff: some of them are much, much older. But that is the greatest of the rooms."

Remembering a visit I had paid to the Dordogne area a few months before, I inquired if any wall paintings or rock carvings had been found in these Seine valley caves. He replied that he did not think so; he certainly had not heard of them. Plenty of instruments of flint, yes, and of the horns of the deer for digging, yes, but not the paintings or the sculpture. He thought it was only in the south that such things had been found.

Strangely enough, it was the cassowary, a bird inhabiting islands in the Western Pacific, that sent me to the Dordogne in search of prehistoric paintings. I was in London at the time and had been reading of this bird's method of fishing, and I thought to get a clearer picture of its features by a visit to the Natural History Museum at South Kensington. Observers tell us that when hungry it walks into the water and then, partially squatting, opens its rudimentary wings and ruffles its feathers, submerging all but its head and neck. For perhaps a quarter of an hour it will remain in that position, motionless, as if asleep. Then suddenly it will contract its plumage and step ashore. No sooner on dry land than it gives itself a violent shake, whereupon numbers of small fish fall to the ground. The rest is easy.

I looked at this emu-like bird in its case and noted the heavy black plumage. The feathers were of the primitive type, resembling coarse hair. When expanded under water they would make wonderful cover for small fish, and if the bird had parasites they might supply food as well. I admired, too, its blue and crimson wattled neck, and noticed the powerful legs with the enormous development of the inner claws of its three-toed feet. If a kick from a kiwi weighing six pounds can cut you to the bone, what would result, I wondered, from the kick of a cassowary weighing maybe 160 pounds?

And then as I passed through the central hall I met my friend Dr. F. C. Fraser of the museum.

"Come and look at our new exhibit," he said, leading me to one of the side galleries. Stags' antlers, flint and stone implements. "Mesolithic," said Fraser, "about 8000 B.C., one of the richest and most informative sites of the Maglemosian culture in Western Europe. Links up with the cultures of that period in Denmark and Esthonia—of course, you could walk from Yorkshire to Esthonia till about 6000 B.C., when the sea encroached."

In the case before me were shown antlers that had been used as clubs and mattocks; there were tines from the antlers that had been bevelled for use as chisels or wedges; there were rolls of birch bark similar to those stored by Swedish Laplanders today for flooring or for making containers; there were harpoon-like points, or spear-heads, from a few inches to a foot in length, with many barbs, made from strips of the antlers. Flint burins exhibited alongside worked antlers showed how the strips had been cut. And perhaps most exciting to the imagination, there was the frontal bone of a red deer with holes bored through it for attachment to something, human or otherwise. The antlers had been split and hollowed and shaven, so that little of their weight remained. They might have been worn in a ritual dance, they might have been used by hunters when stalking their quarry.

Fraser took me downstairs to his semi-subterranean quarters in the museum, and it was when he was showing me other specimens from the same find that I noticed on his desk a copy of a book by Fernand Windels describing the wall paintings at Lascaux. It was a large volume with many coloured plates: horses, oxen, reindeer, in red, black and yellow, charging about the walls of a hundred-foot long grotto.

"You'd think they hadn't been painted twenty years," said Fraser.

"And how old are they?" I asked.

"About twenty thousand years," he said.

I read from one of the pages before me: "When one enters the caves at Lascaux the first impression is of going into a majestic sanctuary."

"And your last impression is of having been in one," said Fraser. "The place is almost overpowering. I've just come back. It was only discovered about ten years ago," he added, "when some young people playing in the woods lost their dog. It had fallen through a small hole into a cave, and when they squeezed through the hole to rescue the animal this was what they found."

Cassowaries that had been paddling in my mind earlier in the day now disappeared into the bush.

"You must go to Les Eyzies," continued Fraser, "and stay at the Cro-Magnon Hotel—you couldn't find better. That's where the remains of the Cro-Magnon people were first found. From there you can visit half a dozen other grottoes as well."

He was right. The Cro-Magnon is one of the pleasantest small hotels that I met during my travels in France. Food, wine, friendship and everything else that one needs, in simple perfection. Like many other houses in the district it is built under an overhanging cliff, so much so that on the staircase and along the corridors a wall is often the naked rock. It was explained to me that in the local patois *cro* means hole and *magnon* means big; it is a country of caves and grottoes, of large holes. The skull that many believe to be one of the links, no longer missing, from the human chain, takes its name from the district in which it was found. It is gargantuan country: one feels that in it a mammoth would be no more noticeable than a snipe in a bog. On either side of the river monstrous cliffs, ice-worn in another age, overhang the paths and the dwellings of man. In such a setting humanity is insignificant. One can imagine puny human cries echoing faintly across the valley and ant-like fights to the death at the fords, but the bloodstained water would quickly carry away the tiny corpses and soon there would be no more memory of the struggle than there is today of a mole or a field-mouse crushed by a passing car.

On my first morning I visited the grotto of Le Grand Roc, much advertised. No paintings here, just natural formations. Three hundred yards of galleries winding their undetermined ways deep into the entrails of the earth. Skin-tight corridors serpentining through vistas of stalagmites and stalactites that glittered on the floor like stage jewels among crystallized fruit, or hung from the roof like tipsy chandeliers.

In the afternoon I went to Les Combarelles, another tortuous tunnel, low and narrow, with shiny scabrous walls and dripping roof. No paintings here either, but scratchings in profusion, outlines of animals graven on the walls, of mammoth, wolf, bear, ibex, bison; an occasional fish: almost an inventory of the fauna of the land as it existed twenty thousand years ago. Looking at the portrait of the mammoth, it was strange to think that today in Siberia they are still finding bodies of these animals so preserved in the ice, even after perhaps a hundred thousand years or more, that the flesh, like frozen beef, can be fed to dogs who devour it with relish. So thorough has been the natural refrigeration of the bodies that from fragments of food found between the teeth it has been possible to ascertain with certainty the diet of these animals—leaves of willow, pine and fir, flowers and grass.

Why primitive man crawled into the inner recesses of dripping caves to scrape with infinite patience upon the walls is a matter for conjecture. The general opinion seems to be that the drawings are connected with some form of propitiatory magic, with rites that would ensure successful hunting; but in contradiction of this there is a cave near Bordeaux where from the evidence of bone remains the inhabitants hunted mammoth, rhinoceros and the great elk, yet the only animals depicted by them on their walls are domestic ones—goats, horses and an ox. There is also another cave further south, at Marsoulas, where an abundance of reindeer bones has been found about the hearths, but only one picture of a reindeer, and that a doubtful one, on the walls.

Lascaux lies about fifteen miles by road from Les Eyzies; the final approach to the cave is by a sandy path through a pine wood. Until the actual entrance has been reached there is nothing to suggest that anything but solid earth lies below the surface, no hint whatever that such a temple could exist beneath one's feet.

From the daylight by a few broad steps one descends into semi-darkness; the ground becomes moist and water seeps from the rock overhead. There is a second door to be thrown open, and then before one's eyes, around the sides and over the roof of the great domed cave, there flows a fantastic panorama of bellowing bulls, charging bisons, reindeer and horses. Ponies gallop across the walls, untamed cattle come to a sudden halt with the fear of death or capture in their eyes, or drop

pierced by arrows. The artists have taken advantage of natural formations—a prominence or a bulge of rock may be the head or rounded belly of a beast. There is no drawing to scale: each animal or group of animals is relative only to the area it covers. The designs of succeeding generations often overlap each other, and that without detriment or incongruity, indeed with but added emphasis. The drawing of the individual animals is superb: only men as conversant with their habits as a herdsman with those of his cattle could have depicted them with such incisiveness of line, with such appreciation of form, with such vitality of movement. The colours used were the natural ones beneath their feet: red and yellow earth, compact enough to be cut into pencils, black granulous soil for the deeper tones. Their brushes may have been the bristles on a scrap of hide, or for the wider areas a tuft of moss or lichen. The artists may at times have blown the pigment on to the rock through a hollow stem.

From the main court of the grotto a passage on the right leads into a second hall. The walls of the passage are covered with engravings of ibex and stags, the hall is as richly decorated in colour as the main court. In it there is a superb frieze of stags' heads, drawn as though the beasts were swimming through a torrent. From this hall in one direction there opens *le cabinet des felins*, where cave-lions are the theme of the engraving; in another direction a ladder, at a sudden change of level, drops one into "the well," a narrow and still but partly explored cavern.

Here a bird-headed man is prostrate before an infuriated bison; near by is an unfinished but splendid two-horned rhinoceros. In a smaller gallery, opening almost directly from the main court, stocky little ponies in varied colours dominate the scene.

Wherever one stands in the caves the effect on the mind is the same—overwhelming. Those early men of Lascaux have left little that tells us of their daily lives—a few cut flints, a few hollowed stones that held colour for the artists or animal fat for "household" lighting. But they have left an awesome sanctuary, the most impressive picture gallery that I have ever entered.

# CHAPTER TWENTY-SIX

FROM thoughts of prehistoric hunters and unlettered lives there came a sudden change to notions of great sophistication. A mile down river from the subterranean church, we passed the ancient fortress of Roche Guyon, built on the cliff side by a seigneur named Guyon. Today it belongs to descendants of the famous Duc de la Rochefoucauld, whose *Maximes*, according to Voltaire, "contributed more to form the taste of the French nation, and give it a true relish of propriety and correctness, than any other performance." A few of them at random:

> We should often be ashamed of our best actions, if the world saw *all* their motives.
> The generality of friends puts us out of conceit with friendship, and the generality of religious people makes us out of conceit with religion.
> There are women who never had an intrigue; but there are scarce any who never had but one.
> Gravity is a mysterious carriage of the body, invented to cover the defects of the mind.
> Jealousy is the greatest of evils, and the least pitied by those who occasion it.
> The love of justice is in most men only the fear of suffering by injustice.

Clear thinking, perfection of phrasing, but grim. What a genius the French have for maxims and *pensées*: Pascal on religion, Joubert on literary criticism, Chamfort on human character; and La Rochefoucauld, the greatest of all, in devastating words stripping every illusion from the motives of human conduct. Many of his maxims must shock those of romantic temperament, and many even of realistic temperament will gulp before admitting their truth. From his pages one would gather that the author was a man whose soul was filled with disdain for his fellow creatures. And yet Madame de Sévigné who knew him well wrote: "I have never seen a man so obliging nor more amiable in his wish to give pleasure by what he says." Embittered by his life at a court where insincerity and sycophancy were the ruling monarchs, the duke at the age of forty retired to the country, resolved to extirpate these festerings with the scalpel of his wit. It was a love of truth rather than a hatred of mankind that forced him to an almost excessive cynicism.

It would be pleasant to quote other epigrams from those whose names I have mentioned, but this alone from Chamfort is a stern deterrent: "Some people," he says, "put their books into their library, but Monsieur—puts his library into his books." I will therefore allow myself but one more, a kindly one from Joubert: "When my friends lack an eye, I look at them in profile." I agree: concentrating one's thoughts on the imperfections of others is as sterile as self-pity.

Heavy storm clouds were banking in the sky when Château Gaillard hove in sight, silver as the cliff on which it stands. The skipper put the engine to slow while I made a hurried drawing.

This castle was built by Richard Coeur de Lion during the years 1195–8. Perched on its precipice, it was thought to be impregnable. Richard, viewing his completed work, remarked: "Que voilà un château gaillard!" A gallant castle indeed, and hence the name.

When Philippe-Auguste, King of France, heard of this fortress within what he considered to be his own dominion, he was far from pleased. "Were it built of iron," he said testily, "I would still take it, and with it restore Normandy to France." Richard, hearing of this, retorted: "Had it been built of butter, I would still defend it against him and his." Philippe-Auguste did eventually take the castle, though not from Coeur de Lion who had died five years earlier. In March 1204, after a siege of many months, French troops penetrated to the heart of the citadel and

captured the last of the English defenders, "one hundred and fifty, of whom forty were knights." Bayeux, Rouen and other towns fell soon after. Normandy was lost to England.

But that was not the end of the château's part in history. More than two hundred years later, in 1418, the troops of Henry V of England laid siege to it, a siege that lasted sixteen months before the French garrison surrendered. Then, twelve years later, after a daring assault commanded by one Captain La Hire, the French flag was again flying over the *donjon.* Within another year the English were once more in command, and so the struggle continued until in 1449 the French came finally into possession. Today the towers are roofless, the moats have fallen in, the battlements have crumbled, but wild flowers and sweet-smelling herbs self-sown among the ruins mingle their fragrance on that oft-disputed hill.

The river widened and swung to the left. On our starboard bow the village of Petit Andely lay at the entrance to a wooded valley; beyond it among the hills its sister, Grand Andely. "Les Andelys," said the pilot, "le lieu natal de Poussin."

The French are very proud of their painters. I told him of two of Poussin's canvases which hang alongside each other in the National Gallery in London. In one of them, *Bacchanalian Revel*, the central group is of three figures dancing; there is a lady on the left draped in blue, there is a gentleman on the right wearing a golden loin-cloth, and between them another gentleman who wears nothing. When we look at the other picture, *The Worship of the Golden Calf*, we find the same three people in almost exactly the same poses, but now they are, as in a mirror, reversed. The male figure in the centre of the group is no longer naked but wears a garment of indigo blue embroidered with gold; the lady, formerly on the left, is now on the right in a dark green skirt, while the third member of the party, apart from putting on a wreath of vine leaves, has changed little except for the lighting on his body.

"Poussin would have seen much dancing at Les Andelys when he was a boy," said the pilot. "In that time the people were possessed by the dance. In the *salons*, in the streets, always, always the dance. The town was very *célèbre* for its cancans."

The clouds had passed, the sky was clear, the glare from the water was intense and I had sat on my sun glasses. The worst of a ship with a screw and a crew is that when you see a beach, a sand-bank or a meadow inviting to the feet or the seat you cannot go ashore. Inexorably the propeller turns, rushing you past every terrestrial seduction, as a maiden aunt might hurry her nephew past a window show of lingerie. The river below Les Andelys was veined with coppiced islets. I would fain have rested in their shade. Instead, having happened on the tattered Pan edition of Slocum's voyaging that was on board, I glanced at it to rest my eyes. The pages described his seventy-two solitary days at sea between Juan Fernandez and Samoa. "I had already found," he writes, "that it was not good to be alone, and so I made companionship with what there was around me, sometimes with the universe and sometimes with my own insignificant self; but my books were always my friends, let fail all else." He had so perfectly contrived the balance of his gear that his sloop would sail herself. No need for him to be at the tiller day or night. Sometimes he would awake to hear the water rushing by with only a thin plank between him and the depths, and he would say: "How is this?" Then he would realize that it was *his* ship on *her* course, "sailing as no other ship had ever sailed before in the world ... I knew that no human hand was at the helm; I knew that all was well with 'the hands' forward, and that there was no mutiny on board." He had found the secret of a happy life—to contrive the balance of one's gear and let no hand but one's own control the helm.

# CHAPTER TWENTY-SEVEN

As we approached the village of Poses, smooth hillsides intersected by valleys sloped to the water's edge. Here and there white scars where land had slipped showed strata upon strata of chalk—the fore edges of leaves in a mighty history book. Just below the village was our last lock, a deeper basin than most of the others we had passed through, with a difference of some eighteen to twenty feet between levels. As we sank slowly between oozing walls, watching the small jets of water that spurted from cavities behind the slimy stones, a lady clambered on board, entered the wheel-house without knocking and embraced the pilot. He introduced her to us as his wife. They had lived in Poses for many years, he said.

Madame was very appreciative of the fact that I was writing about the Seine. "The district around here in particular," she said, "is one of the most beautiful by the river. Also it is a region that is very privileged for the fisherman. Nobody ever takes home his basket without it being full. The people of the village say it is because the country is so *ravissant* that the fish want to jump out of the water to look at it." As the gates at the far end of the lock opened and we moved forward, Madame herself jumped nimbly on to the lower rungs of an iron ladder set vertically in the wall. Her husband was too busy at the wheel even to wave to her. But what matter? He was leaving us at Rouen and would be home that evening.

We were now in tidal waters and sand-banks in midstream lay uncovered. From one of them a wisp of sandpipers rose and sped downstream; from another a solitary curlew, rising, sounded its lonesome call.

There did not seem to be anything exceptionally "ravissant" near the low left bank of the river where the village lies, but on the other side rose an exceptionally high and precipitous chalk cliff. "La Côte des Deux Amants," said the pilot. Then as he guided us past the many confluences of the river Eure, and towards Elbeuf, he told me the story of that hill, a tale that goes back to the time of the Crusades.

There was living then a rich and powerful seigneur, le Comte Rulph, whose domain extended through the valley of the Andelle, a tributary of the Seine that separates that high spur, la Côte, from its neighbouring hills to the west. The count was a typical bad baron of the story books, cruel and selfish to a degree, and he had a daughter by name Calixte who excelled in the virtues even as he excelled in the vices. He had, too, *un écuyer*, a squire, named Edmond, *un très brave garçon*, as handsome as Calixte was beautiful. The two had been brought up together as children: they were to each other as brother and sister.

One day there came word to the count that a wild boar was devastating the countryside. Next morning hunting-horns echoed in the forest: "*Tai-aut! Tai-aut! Tai-aut!*" And all the chevaliers and their *châtelaines* came to the hunt. Calixte was there too, though she did not like the hunting: she preferred to look at the flowers and to listen to the songs of the birds. That was why she stayed a little way behind the others as they rode through the forest. And then, while she was alone, she heard the horn again: "*Tai-aut! Tai-aut! Tai-aut!*" and she heard the hounds cry, and she knew that *le sanglier* had been found and driven from its haunts. So, because her father would have wished it, she put her horse at the trot to rejoin the hunt. Alas, the horse tripped on the root of a tree and fell, throwing Calixte to the ground. And just then the wild boar rushed from cover followed by the hounds in full cry. Seeing Calixte, it was about to charge when—*soudain, miraculeusement*—Edmond was there! He was between Calixte and the infuriated beast.

Ah, the valiant youth! What did he do? Listen! Gripping his spear with both hands and standing firmly on both feet, he met the onrush with the point of his weapon. He pierced the creature through and through. Blood spurted from it like a fountain. It dropped dead. Then the hero, kneeling beside the prostrate girl, took her in his arms, and for the first time their lips met in love.

Now along comes Count Rulph and his suite. At a glance they take in what has happened—all except the kiss. "*Bel écuyer*," said the count, "ask of me what reward you wish and I shall grant it unto you."

"No other reward but that I may unite my life with that of Calixte," said Edmond.

The count's first answer was a contemptuous laugh. Then his features grew purple with rage. Did the varlet not know that only one of noble rank might hope to wed his daughter?

"I thought by past service to have qualified for knighthood," said Edmond. "Yet true nobility is of the heart."

"Tomorrow, if you are able, you shall qualify for noble rank, and with it for my daughter's hand," said the count. "Tomorrow," he said, "you will climb that spur between the Andelle and the Seine, carrying Calixte on your back. If you stop but one moment for breath you will lose."

"I will do it," said Edmond.

Next morning the two lovers heard mass in the nearby church. *Longtemps ils prolongèrent leurs oraisons*, and then they went to the foot of the hill. A huge crowd had already assembled. All were looking upward at a flag hanging from a pole, six hundred feet above the river. That was the gage.

Edmond took Calixte on his back and began to climb. He kept on his feet in slippery places, he heaved himself over rocks that stood in his way. Never hesitating, he climbed higher and higher. The crowd watched him anxiously. From every château and cottage in the neighbourhood they had come. Now there were but sixty feet to go, now fifty, now thirty. The flag hung limp; Edmond struggled on.

Then from the assembled crowd there came a mighty roar: Edmond held the flag! Incontinently they shouted their delight. Trumpets blared for victory. Edmond had won.

But even as he held the flag, the heart within him burst and he dropped to the ground, dead.

Calixte knelt on the summit of the hill beside him. For a moment she was helpless, stupefied. Then putting forth all her strength she gathered his body into her arms. A few moments later the crowd at the foot of the hill saw two bodies in close embrace come hurtling down the steep slope, somersaulting the boulders in their course. All fled in terror when two corpses rolled at their feet.

Next morning there came to the room where Edmond's body lay a company of nobles and prelates, carrying with them the insignia of knighthood. They put upon Edmond the coat of mail, the helmet and the golden spurs, they laid his sword upon his breast, his shield and lance beside him. Then they gave him the accolade of knighthood. In the next room lay Calixte, in bridal dress. They carried the two bodies to the nearby church and there in one tomb they laid them.

"And what became of the count?" I asked, as the pilot came to the end of his story.

"On ne sait pas," he replied. "But it is said," he added, "that, *accablé de remords*, he founded a monastery for men and a convent for women, and then—because he was afraid for his future, you understand—he joined a crusade and died in the Holy Land. I do not know; but that is the story they tell of the hill—*la légende des deux amants*."

# CHAPTER TWENTY-EIGHT

BELOW Elbeuf, a town given over to industry—wool spinning, dyeing, soap manufacture—there are again the steep green hillsides with their outcrops and buttresses of chalk. Innumerable grottoes, too, from which one could imagine gnomes with dark, deep-set eyes emerging at night to raid the neighbouring fields. In places the great white buttresses are like battered sphinxes guarding their green temples, in others the pillars sculptured by wind and rain stand, aloof from each other, like gigantic chessmen. As we sailed down a long avenue of poplars, factory chimneys and church spires ahead of us heralded Rouen.

Now barges lay thick on either bank, moored in fleets according to their "houses." Many of the black hulls had a coloured bow stripe, heraldic in its import. Some wore azure with two gold stars, others a scarlet and white device that gave to the bows the grin of a Maori mask. Some carried stripes of orange and white, others of scarlet and blue. Their names, too, were indicative of their clans: I saw *Nile, Rhône, Loire,* together at one quay; at another, where zoology was preferred, the *Bison, Lama, Zebra, Camel* and *Gazelle*; at another the *Caucase*, the *Anglais*, the *Algérie.*

Tall cranes hedged the river, yellow and black, bowing and curtsying in all directions. A large ship in dry dock rose from the fields; a small ship hung in a network of derricks like a fly caught in a web. Ships from Norway, Denmark, England, Ireland, Italy, were alongside the quays, unloading and loading coal and timber and grain. Voices in many languages shouted orders, or called from deck to deck.

"There was a Russian ship here last trip," said Slim, "an' there wasn't a man on board her—whole ship worked by women. I reckon they were good, too. During the war I saw Russian women loading torpedoes, and they did it in half the time it took the men."

The wharves seemed very full as we made our way along. There wasn't room for even a hard-boiled egg between bow and stern of any two ships that lay alongside, let alone a hundred feet of *Yarvic*. We feared we might have to anchor in the stream and hope for better luck next day—we couldn't go further without clearance papers. Slim was singing a snatch of his favourite song:

*If ever devil's plan*
*Was made to torment man*
*It was you, Jezebel, it was you.*

Just when all hope was fading the pilot spotted a vacant berth and, with the delight of the child that flops into the last seat in a game of musical chairs, swung us about and alongside.

Now his term of office was completed; he said good-bye and hurried away. It was getting late and he had to make his way back to his wife and home at Poses. For us, we would spend the night where we were and in the morning get our papers and take a new pilot aboard.

No sooner had all these decisions been reached than the harbour-master appeared. He said we were to move at once. A large ship was expected at any moment: she had been promised our position and there wasn't room for us both. He didn't know where else we could go, but we were certainly to move and that *immédiatement.* He would listen to no argument. He even threatened us with a tug.

Slim greeted the news with his usual guffaw and went ashore. We could see him talking to the captain of the Dutch ship that lay directly ahead of us. A little later he brought the captain along the quay and suggested we should offer him a drink. Our skipper passed a large glass of brandy through the window of the wheel-house. The Dutchman emptied the glass with a single delicate gesture and then came aboard to join us. Slim poured him a glass of neat rum. He dealt with that as gracefully as he had dealt with the brandy. "Why yes," he said, "there would be no difficulty." He would slacken his hawsers and we could slip in between his ship and the quay. We could lie abreast till he sailed at midnight, and then the berth would be ours. Would we not come on board his ship now and drink some Hollands Gin? We thanked him, but excused ourselves with a "next time" promise. Our ship had to be moved, and then we were going into the town. "Next time, then, in Paris—the Quai d'Austerlitz," said the Dutchman. "My wife come from Birmingham—she speak good English."

An hour later, in the gathering dusk, Peters and I made our way into the town. There was an air of fantasy about everything; ghostly figures moved among ruins haunted by the spectres of destruction. Narrow dark streets led from one area of desolation to another. If through a café window one glimpsed a smiling face, it had even less reality than the slinking shadows in the streets. At any moment the grotesque contours of shattered architecture might resolve themselves into semi-human forms, at any moment one might hear the phrenetic cry of zombies echoing from the cratered pavements. It needed the inside of a restaurant to bring us back to actuality.

Next morning, while the captain dealt with officials, I had time for a hurried walk through the town. From the quay, its rail lines and its derricks, by way of avenues through set-square skeletons of contemporary architecture now arising, I reached the cathedral square. Here, dominating all else, was the great Gothic façade that Monet had painted so often—twenty times at least—realizing on each canvas a different effect of light, a different harmony of colour. *Plein Soleil, Effet du Matin, Soleil Matinal, Temps Gris*: blues and golds and purples, rose tints and apple greens, he had found them all in this ash-grey filigree of stone. Monet, like the other Impressionists, was more concerned with the momentary effect of light and colour than in the inherent properties of the subject itself. When living at Giverny he painted the same stretch of the Seine under eighteen different atmospheric conditions; when he visited London he painted the Houses of Parliament eleven times, concentrating not on the architecture but on its appearance through river fogs. He made forty-eight compositions of water-lilies and their reflections.

From the cathedral, still closed to the public for repair, I turned west into the Rue du Gros Horloge and, passing under the big gilt clock with its sun-rayed dial telling the time of day and above it a globe telling the phase of the moon, I made my way to the market-place. There, on the very site where in 1431 Joan of Arc was burned, is now held every morning *le marché aux fleurs*. It is as though the citizens wished that always there should be flowers at her feet.

# CHAPTER TWENTY-NINE

I WONDER how many card players in England know that the designs they hold in their hands are derived from the patterns of cards manufactured in Rouen. I didn't know myself till I had visited the city. Apart from St. Bernard of Siena and an Elizabethan Puritan, John Northbrooke, who attributed their invention to the devil, no one is quite sure where or whence the pack originated. But we do know that playing-cards seem to have been invented about six hundred years ago, that for several centuries France was the chief card-making nation in Europe and that in the seventeenth century card-making was one of the most important trades in Rouen. Their manufacture in England did not begin until about 1450.

In France from the first the court cards were given names, and on many modern packs the names still appear. The King of Hearts was Charlemagne, the great emperor. The Queen of Hearts was the biblical figure Judith, because of her courage and "good heart." At first the Knave of Hearts, the *Valet de Coeur*, appeared as a somewhat effeminate youth, but from the seventeenth century he has been none other than the Captain La Hire who captured Château Gaillard from Richard Coeur de Lion. A romantic figure, if somewhat undisciplined, Shaw in *St. Joan* calls him "a war dog with no court manners and pronounced camp ones"; Anatole France in his life of Joan of Arc refers to him as "the most valiant man in France."

It is told by a fifteenth-century writer that one morning in the year 1427, just before going into an attack against the English in which the odds were heavily against him, La Hire sought absolution from a priest.

"But first you must confess," said the priest.

"There is no time," said La Hire.

The priest was insistent.

"You may take it," said La Hire, "that I have committed every sin common to soldiers." The priest still demurred, but eventually granted his request, stipulating that afterwards he should offer a prayer. La Hire then, kneeling, prayed, "O God, I pray Thee to do for La Hire today such things as Thou wouldst wish La Hire to do for Thee, if he were God, and if Thou wert La Hire," a prayer that will remind many of the well-known epitaph:

*Here lie I, Martin Elginbrodde;*
*Hae mercy o' my soul, Lord God;*
*As I wad do, were I Lord God,*
*And ye were Martin Elginbrodde.*

George Macdonald in his novel *David Elginbrod* attributes this epitaph to a churchyard in Aberdeen, but in fact it appears to have been parodied from one on a tombstone in Dundee. The notion, however, is not a new one, nor limited to Scotland. Germany, Switzerland and Ireland have all had their versions. A similar thought occurred to an Indian poet three thousand years ago, when he wrote: "If I, O Indra, were like thee, the only lord of wealth, he who praised me should not lack cows."

In modern French cards the King of Spades is David with his harp and sword; the King of Diamonds is Julius Caesar; the King of Clubs is Alexander the Great. Among the queens are the biblical Rachel and the pagan Minerva Pallas; among the knaves are Sir Hector of the Round Table and Sir Launcelot of the Lake. Others who from time to time have made their appearance include Cleopatra, Bathsheba, King Arthur, Joan of Arc, and Helen of Troy; but for a full account of these and other personages, and the reasons for their presence at the cardboard court, I would refer the reader to Mr. Gurney Benham's history of the pack, *Playing Cards.*

About seven miles below Rouen, on the right bank of the river, stands the bronze eagle that commemorates the transference from one ship to another of the body of Napoleon, on the final stage of its homeward journey from St. Helena. Napoleon had expressed a wish that after his death his remains should be brought back to France and buried beside the Seine. In his will he had written: "Je désire que mes cendres reposent sur les bords de la Seine, au milieu de ce peuple français que j'ai tant aimé." ["I wish that my ashes should rest on the banks of the Seine, amidst that French people whom I have so loved"]. But when he died in 1821 the English Government, for political reasons, would not allow his body to be taken from the island—it had been decided in 1817 and confirmed in 1820 that the burial was to take place on St. Helena, "with the military honours due to an English General." Only in 1840 was permission obtained to bring the body home to Paris. Palmerston, then Foreign Secretary, though acceding to the request, thought it "very French."

Two ships, the frigate *Belle-Poule* and the corvette *La Favorite*, commanded by the Prince de Joinville, third son of the king, Louis-Philippe, sailed from Toulon in July of the same year; they reached St. Helena three months later. At midnight of the 14th October the exhumation began. It was drizzling and cold with faint glimmers of moonlight. Soldiers of the 91st Regiment, now the 1st Battalion of the Argyll and Sutherland Highlanders, in their red coats, held lanterns and torches. Iron railings, flowering plants and flagstones had to be removed. It wasn't till four o'clock in the morning that they reached the masonry of the tomb: it wasn't till half past nine that the outer coffin of mahogany could be seen, the heads of its silver screws shining in the rain. A priest, l'Abbé Coquereau, who had come with the expedition from France, sprinkled holy water and recited the *De Profundis*. Then the fourfold coffin was lifted—two casings of wood, two of metal. It was carried to a tent, and the same workman who twenty years before had soldered the inner lining now cut it open with his chisels.

"Napoleon seemed to sleep." Those present had expected to find little more than a skeleton: instead, they saw the face of their emperor, almost unchanged. Without a grey hair, without a wrinkle; except that his skin had darkened slightly, he was as they had seen him on the day of his death. Even his dress was scarcely affected; the ribbon of the Légion d'Honneur that lay on his breast was as new, only the gold of his epaulettes was a little tarnished. Those of his contemporaries who had come back to fetch him were now old men; the emperor had remained young.

There was no need for further identification. The coffins were sealed again.

That evening at six o'clock Napoleon left St. Helena, twenty-five years to the hour since he had landed there. It was recorded that the only ray of sunlight that lit the sea that pouring day broke through the clouds as the British cannons fired their farewell salute.

On 29th November the *Belle-Poule* arrived at Cherbourg and the coffin was transferred to a smaller ship, *La Normandie*, which brought it up the Seine as far as Le Val de la Haye. There, where the bronze eagle now marks the site, the body was put on board a yet smaller vessel, *La Dorade*, and on her deck the emperor completed his homeward journey and re-entered his capital. In his darkest hours on St. Helena he had said to his companions: "You will yet hear Paris cry, 'Vive l'Empereur!'" Now, as the cortège passed through the streets, a million voices acclaimed him. Even the saluting guns were muted by the shouting.

Mention of the Napoleonic eagle recalls a pleasant incident described by Monsieur André Billy, from whom I have quoted in another context. This time, in his book *Le Pont des Saints Pères*, he tells of a visit to England by a party of distinguished French authors, organized by Charles Saroléa, then Professor of French Literature in Edinburgh University. It was in the spring of 1914. "At Folkestone," writes Monsieur Billy, "we had a foretaste of British hospitality. In our honour there was a march past of the garrison: Highlanders, artillery, cavalry. In the principal street of the town the parade was astonishing: there could not have been greater ceremony for a sovereign." But the highlight of the entertainment for the visitors was when the band of the Royal Irish Fusiliers, drawn up on a lawn, played the *Marseillaise* "with pious slowness." It was after this that Monsieur Billy, noticing an eagle of Napoleon on the drum-major's staff, inquired how it came to be there. "'Tis the way we were after taking it from the French," was the reply.

It was during the Peninsular War that in 1811 at the battle of Barrosa this eagle of the French 8th Regiment of Infantry was captured by the

Fusiliers. The moral importance of its capture was immense, for it was one of those eagles given by Napoleon himself to his troops a few days after his coronation. He had decreed that every battalion of foot, every squadron of horse, every battery of artillery, even every ship of the line, should have its own eagle, and he himself would present them. This Eagle of the Caesars, this "Eagle with the golden wreath," was to be the Standard of the French Empire. Before a vast throng of spectators, on the Champ de Mars in Paris, forty thousand troops with one mighty roar swore to their emperor that they would defend the symbol with their lives. The 8th Regiment because of its prowess in battle was singled out for special distinction: whereas the eagles of all the other corps could be unscrewed from their shafts in moments of danger, that of the 8th Regiment was permanently attached. "From such a regiment," said Napoleon, "it could not be taken." But the men from Galway, Clare and Tipperary, finding themselves outnumbered by three to one on that hill in the south of Spain, fixed bayonets and charged. Colonel Autié kept his oath to Napoleon and gave his life in defending the eagle. Ensign Keogh gave his in taking it. A leaf that fell from its wreath was picked up later on the field of battle and presented to Major Hugh Gough, then commanding the regiment. Today, known as the Barrosa pendant, it is an heirloom of his family.

# CHAPTER THIRTY

OUR new pilot lacked the geniality of his predecessor. He was morose and uncommunicative, volunteering no information and giving as little as possible when questioned. Neither did he take the wheel, preferring to sit with a book in his hand and throw an occasional curt order to Slim, Tilly, or whoever might be on duty. When, as we passed the ruin of a castle, high on a hill above La Bouille, I inquired if it was the Château of Robert le Diable, father of "the Conqueror," an affirmative grunt was his only reply. When, pertinaciously, I suggested that from what I had heard much of the building was not the original architecture but a recent restoration, a shrug of his shoulders added little to my knowledge. Nor had he anything to say about the little village of La Bouille, whose houses seem thrust forward to the water's edge by the high chalk cliffs behind them. Hotels that might have been in Venice flanked the square, scarce bigger than a stage; a dark Othello with his golden Desdemona stood waiting for the other players to arrive.

A mile below La Mailleraye, with the tide running in our favour, we were making good speed. After a stretch of open country the hills were gathering in again and we expected shortly to pass Caudebec. The pilot gave the order: "Starboard"; Slim at the wheel obeyed. Next moment the *Yarvic* gave three mighty bounds, like the leaps of a greyhound from its leash. Then she stopped, inert as a spaniel before the fire. Slim's particular brand of laugh confirmed my impression that we were aground.

"Une butte," muttered the pilot, which I gathered meant a sand-bank. He added something to the effect that the floods had caused a change in the river-bed. Never before, he said, stabbing with a finger at the chart, had he encountered "une butte" in such a position. Our propeller churned discoloured water but we did not move.

"Tide'll be up in two hours," said Slim cheerfully. He took the megaphone from its hook and whistled through it. "Call up a wind'll blow us off," he said. "Last skipper we had'd never let you whistle on a fine day—said it was calling up the wind. 'Whistle when there's a fog,' he'd say, 'that's the only time we want a wind.'" He put the instrument back on its hook. "An' he wouldn't have a cat aboard neither—bring bad luck, he'd say. An' he wouldn't have no mistletoe in the ship. Someone tied a bit to the mast one Christmas time, an' it was nothing but disaster after. Cap'n said it was all 'n account of the mistletoe."

We settled down to a quiet afternoon. The pilot showed no desire to express himself further; the captain refrained from doing so. A flight of steps on the river-bank marked the falling tide. Tilly and Pullen went forward to grease hawsers; Rowden went into the galley to brew tea. Slim's whistling was having its effect—the wind was rising.

Time passed. The sympathetic captain of a passing barge brought his vessel alongside and tried to tow us off, but with no success. If only a tug would come along, we thought—we had seen enough of them at Rouen. But never a sight of one now.

Tea arrived through the hole in the deck. It was only when we were sending back the empty cups that we noticed the tide had turned. Now clouds were racing across the sky, and spatters of rain reminded us of a falling barometer.

Another half-hour went by. The cook made his appearance to discuss the menu for dinner. Had we any particular tin in mind that we would like opened? Did we wish any change from mashed potatoes? I remembered an hotel in Dublin where I once spent a fortnight. Twice a day and every day the taters on the menu there had a different title. There were *Pommes Duchesse, Pommes à la Reine, Pommes God-knows what,* and every time it was the same good old *Pommes Nature*—spuds boiled in their skins.

There was plenty of time for contemplation but little in the landscape to inspire it. All the way from Paris I had been conscious of the isolation from the countryside that was inevitable in our mode of travel. We had passed by villages and farms yet known nothing of the inhabitants except that in their seasons they would enjoy or suffer the pleasures or pains common to us all. Now curtains of rain emphasized our isolation. A moorhen in a world of its own bobbed and clucked among some tangled grasses by the bank.

Just before six o'clock we got the weather report from London and with it a gale warning for the Channel, and then as we were listening to the news that followed we felt a tremor in our hull. All eyes turned and looked across the river to the flight of steps, our landmark, and immediately the economic crisis was forgotten. We were shifting. The pilot grunted and laid aside his book; the skipper put his hand to a switch. Slim, already below, did something with the engine, and as if we had never paused we were moving into midstream and on our course again.

It was at Villequier, five miles below the scene of this enforced halt, that in 1843 Victor Hugo's daughter Léopoldine was drowned. With her husband, to whom she had been married but a few months, and two friends she was on the river in a small sailing boat. It was a breathless afternoon; the sails hung limp. Suddenly a squall from the hills hit them and the boat overturned. Not one of the four occupants was saved.

Hugo was fond of all his children but particularly so of Léopoldine: he spoke of her as "the half of his life and of his heart." And now she was dead. So stricken was he that for ten years he almost ceased to write. Thirteen years later, when his *Contemplations* was published, there appeared the poem *À Villequier,* a poignant psalm of resignation, not unmingled with reproach. It had been begun in 1844 but was not completed until 1847. My translation is but a shadow of a few of its lines.

*Now that Paris, its pavements and its statues, its haze and its roofs, are far from my eyes; now that I am under trees, and can think on the beauty of skies; now that I am emerging from the mourning which darkened my soul and can feel nature's own peace enter into my being; now that, sitting at the river's edge, quickened by this serene horizon I can contemplate the wild flowers in the meadows and seek within myself for ultimate truths. Now, oh God, that I have gained the strength henceforth to look upon the stone under whose shadow I know she sleeps for ever... calmed, I bring to you the fragments of this heart, so full of your glory, that you have broken...*

*I know that you have else to do than please us all, and that a child dying, to the anguish of its mother, is of little count to you, to you. I know that fruit falls in the wind, that feathers must drop from birds and flowers lose their scent, that creation is one great wheel which cannot move without crushing someone, something. Months, days, waves of the sea, eyes that weep, all come and go under a blue sky. Grass must grow and children die. O God! I know it all.*

At Villequier the rain had become a deluge and we were due to change pilots once more. No one shed tears as our departing expert bid us a morose good-bye and climbed into a small rowing-boat that had come to fetch him. Ten minutes later his successor stepped on board from a launch, and came into the wheel-house in oilskins dripping as if he had swum in them from the shore. He took the garments off, hung them on a peg, and presented to our view as dapper a young man as you might meet in the Rue Faubourg St. Honoré. Instinctively the captain fastened the buttons of his jacket and I became conscious of a lack of tie. This new director of our fortunes spoke excellent English; he had been an interpreter during the war. He asked if we intended to proceed to Le Havre that evening. Even in such weather there would be no difficulty about the navigation—there were beacons all the way—but with the weather prospects as they were we would almost certainly be held up in Le Havre next day. He suggested that it would be more comfortable to stay where we were for the night. The captain agreed. The pilot then moved us to a mooring out of the course of passing ships, put on his wet oilskins once more, and disappeared over the side. He would be back at eight o'clock next morning.

The rain drenched down on to deck and wheel-house, and spluttered through leaks in the window frames. It was growing dark and lights from the houses in Villequier glittered across the river. Tilly

had set our own riding lights, a white at bow and stern, a red above the wheel-house. The captain arranged "anchor watches," two hours each through the night.

Dinner came up from below—sausages from a tin and mashed potatoes. We turned on an electric heater and the wheel-house became warm and cosy. After a final gale warning from London we heard the announcement of a Sibelius symphony on the Home Service. But there was also dance music from the Light Programme, the Dialogues of Plato from the Third, rumbas from Andorra and Handel from Paris. With Slim's manipulation of the keyboard we got them all—a kind of musical montage. Occasionally the lights of another ship would float past us in the darkness. Occasionally we would hear above the clamour the owl-like hooting of a distant barge.

"Next stop Havre," said the captain as we turned in.

This was to be my last night on the river. Four hundred miles from source to mouth—just twice the length of the Thames. There was scarcely a yard of it that I hadn't touched, from its first cress-bordered trickle to the broad highways where cyclopean buttresses of chalk hold back the hills. As I dropped to sleep my bunk became a boat and the air seemed once again full of catkin fluff, as it had been in the upper reaches. Water glided over trailing weed on either side of me, and swirled under overhanging bushes. Dark stems of trees stretched upwards, infinitely tall, their outline wavy as reflections in a stream.

Just before I awoke next morning I dreamt that, still in my boat, I was making my way through long and tortuous tunnels faintly lit by coloured glass, until I found myself in a vast cathedral whose walls were resplendent with paintings of stags and charging bulls. It seemed odd that as I opened my eyes I should hear the trampling of their hoofs overhead. Then I realized that all hands but my own were on deck and busy.

The weather had changed little overnight: perhaps rather less rain, perhaps rather more wind. The pilot came aboard in good time and joined us at breakfast. He was wearing a gay check suit, white socks, and highly polished brown brogues. He dipped the rather stale bread into his tea without great enthusiasm.

We sailed at eight o'clock. Richly wooded slopes on the left bank were tinged with bronze, "the first clash of autumn's cymbals." Soon the river was winding its course through wide marshes edged on either side with a ribbon of grey mud. Once the whole area had been covered by the sea, but dikes and drainage had converted it to pleasant grazing lands. Wider and wider spread the water, heavier and heavier fell the rain. We passed a dredger at work. "Friends of ours," said Slim. "Give us a basket of fish last time we was here—flounders 'n dabs. Fetches 'em up with the mud."

The scene before us was grey and featureless as a clean slate. If momentarily a chalky smudge appeared, it was the crest of a breaking wave, for now we were crossing and re-crossing the estuary, threading our way between buoys through a channel that grew more and more narrow in an ever-widening river. We had begun to pitch. Ahead of us large ships lay waiting to come into harbour. On our port bow we could see Honfleur whence in 1603 Samuel de Champlain set out to found Quebec and became the first Governor of Canada; and just when I had begun to think that from the way we were heading our destination might well be Nova Scotia, the pilot gave an order to Slim who was at the wheel. Next moment everything that had been standing on the table was rolling or sliding on the floor, and right before us lay the calm waters of Le Havre-de-Grâce.

"Last time I was here," I said to the pilot, "was in 1917. There was snow on the ground and we were in tropical kit, and we froze all the way to Salonique. When we arrived the snow was on the ground there too, and a cutting wind was blowing from Mount Olympus."

"And where are you going to this time?" asked the pilot. "There are no bugles sounding from Mount Olympus today."

"No," I said, "but there are trumpets calling from Montparnasse."

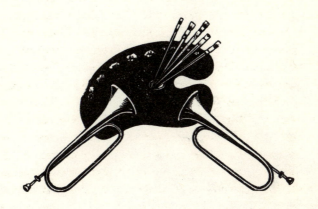